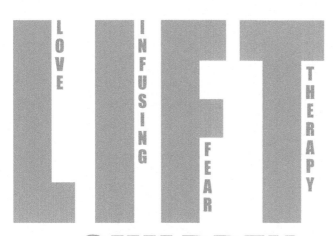

LOVE INFUSING FEAR THERAPY

LIFT

FOR CHILDREN

LIFT
LOVE **I**NFUSING **F**EAR **T**HERAPY

FOR CHILDREN

Unlock Your Child's Full Potential
by Removing Fear and Anger
from Everyday Conflict

Gary M. Unruh, MSW

Lighthouse Love Productions, LLC
Monument, CO

First printing 2021
ISBN 978-0-9824204-5-4

ATTENTION CORPORATIONS, UNIVERSITIES, COLLEGES, AND PROFESSIONAL ORGANIZATIONS: Quantity discounts are available on bulk purchases of this book for educational, gift purposes, or as premiums for increasing magazine subscriptions or renewals. Special books or book excerpts can also be created to fit specific needs. For information, please contact Lighthouse Love Productions, LLC, 18550 Lower Lake Road, Monument, CO 80132.

www.garyunruhtherapy.com

TABLE OF CONTENTS

INTRODUCTION

SEEING YOUR CHILD'S FULLY realized potential? DONE—
if you choose LIFT pioneering tools.

Here is the life-changing, never-before revealed parenting dis-
covery making it all possible:

> Successfully handling daily conflict's fear
> and its anger power source.

That sounds strange, I know. It took me most of my 50-year
counseling career listening carefully to over four thousand children's
precious hearts to get it.

"I did brush my teeth! You never believe..."

*"Your toothbrush is not even wet. If you'd just tell the truth, the
consequences would be way less." You shake your head, eyes closed,
muttering, "Will this never end?"*

Yes, it can end. And where will you find the answer? Your child's
Center, where deep-down feelings that are rarely known and seldom
validated are swirling. This book unveils this Center— the source of
behavior where everything begins—and Love's home, just waiting
to diffuse unnecessary fear and anger. LIFT's DIY skills will unfold
your child's potential right before your eyes every day.

Love's most priceless result, feeling understood, will be your child's continuous experience. LIFT reveals the secret tool: validated emotions, especially fear and anger during conflict. These emotions are defused, love fills the space, and your child's value is cemented into place.

The Golden Rule's elusive requirement—to love yourself—is repeatedly experienced during conflict and is transformed into a core belief: "I'm lovable." The stage is set for loving your neighbor, life's ultimate happiness source.

At the heart of it all is a choice:

Joining (validation) OR splitting ("You are wrong, I am right") during conflict-producing fear and anger.

Ponder with me several chapter subtitles heard from over 4,000 children who have honored me with their unveiled, Center feelings:

- *Always accept my inside emotions first when I'm bad.*
- *Know your upset makes me feel scared and unsafe, like you'll never love me again.*
- *Listen to and see the deepest part of me so I can learn to be good.*

Isn't it strange that one's inside mental health is not as clear as the inside workings of our physical health? An X-ray is taken to diagnose a broken bone, or we start taking medication when our blood pressure numbers are consistently high. Up until now, parenting technology has not been this clear. It includes listening and seeing a child's deepest inside feelings and thoughts. No wonder parenting is so stressful.

But there is breaking news! LIFT (Love Infusing Fear – Therapy) parenting and mental health treatment has finally updated parenting. Affective Neurology research is the basis—inside feelings (emotions and body sensations) are the cause of all thought and behavior. Thanks Disney, for the *Inside Out* movie visuals!

My five decades of clinical experience eventually revealed our deepest emotions are Love and Fear (accompanied by anger). Fear is mostly unconscious, automatically excessive, and Love requires disciplined activation. They occupy the same space. LIFT ascends love to center stage. The performance is transformational for everyone.

Please love me first, LIFT's hallmark feeling validation, is exactly what you will learn to do—guaranteed! Being loved first when "I'm bad" —well, who wouldn't like that? I have lived it through over 50 years of counseling children and in my own humble parenting of four amazing children and nine "grand" children. I am thrilled to pass on what all of these precious children have taught me.

CHAPTER 1

Your Child's Body Emotions and Behavior: Which is the Chicken? Which is the Egg?

Always accept my inside emotions first when I'm bad.

OUR 4th GRADE COUNSELOR, Ms. Haley, pointed to the egg and then to the sometimes-squawking caged chicken on the table and said, "Does anyone know where this chicken started?"

My hand shot up, "The chicken was once a chick and hatched from an egg. I saw it happen on my grandpa's chicken farm."

"You are right," Ms. Haley said. "Way to go Emma! We are all kind of like an egg. Inside us we have body and emotional feelings. You can't see them, but you sure can feel them. But when the inside feelings happen, they almost always hatch and pop out like a chick from an egg.

"Everyone, pinch the top of your wrist." Several "ouches" rippled through the room.

"Raise your hand if your body feels a little pain." Hands flew into the air.

"If the pain continued, would you feel an emotion, like scared or happy? Which emotion would it be?" A chorus of "scared" filled the room.

She pointed to the egg. "Do you see how there are body feelings and emotions inside us, like the chick is inside the eggshell and can't be seen?" Then she pointed to the chicken. "Did you hear the chickens in the room say ouch; the outside behavior coming from the inside pain and scared emotion?"

That's silly, Ms. Haley, calling all of us chickens.

"So, hurting pain can be from body pinching, or hurt from things like being teased. Can someone give an example of feeling hurt by something painful happening in your life?" she asked.

My best friend, Ava raised her hand. "My dog died yesterday..." She started crying.

Ms. Haley walked quickly over to her and while touching her shoulder said, "That really hurts inside, and you showing it on the outside by crying is exactly normal and okay." Looking to the rest of the class she asked, "How many of you feel an inside aching in your stomach for Becky?" Everyone was nodding their heads with sad faces.

Then my other friend, Liam, raised his hand. "My dad lost his job and I'm really sad and scared."

Ms. Haley said, "That's so sad. I ache inside for you. Right now, I'd like each of you to write one or two sentences about how you feel for Liam and Ava. And Liam and Ava, I'd like you to visit me today in my office. I'll give you the notes from your classmates. Now let's take a minute to write the notes.

"Notice as we write our caring notes, our inside body feels a mixture of ache, bath water warmth, and kindness. Do you think the note writing is a pretty good chicken coming from the egg's inside warmth and love?" All heads nodded.

I couldn't wait to tell Mom about how much fun this class was. How funny, that we all have an egg and a chicken happening in our lives.

Now we know the basic inside and outside parts. This section will give you needed detail about the mechanics of how the inside and outside work together.

Inside Is Always the Starting Point

What a great counselor Ms. Haley is. Stories, visuals, and hands-on learning are the best ways to experience what we can't see or hear but know is there. The children *felt* proof about two inside powerful senses: body and emotion. These two senses are the starting point of everything that "pops out" as behavior. *Feeling* and understanding how something works is half the solution. Isn't it interesting how almost everyone misses these basic mechanics: inside typically unknown body and emotion sensations cause outside behavior?

Three Human Parts: LIFT'S Labels

This egg story shows the result of all the things going on inside the three parts of a human being. Imagine a snowman. Part one is the overall Body. Part two is the Mind (head). Part three is the Center (lower body). Children have a lot of fun with this image. The Body communicates through the five senses. Center is home for feelings and emotions, our affective/feeling world, often unconscious but running full speed. Soul, heart and core are other terms used throughout history for this human part. I choose Center because it seemed to really resonate with kids just like the Joy's Control Center in the *Inside Out* movie.

Mind is where thoughts happen, our cognitive/thinking world. Its purpose is to keep everything balanced and running smoothly. Job #1 is to protect against threats—both physical (for example, being burned from a hot surface) and emotional (being yelled at). We have about 40 thoughts per minute, and those thoughts are typically more negative than positive. This is good for avoiding a lion, but not so good for stopping an arguing teen.

Left unattended, the Mind focuses on the negative parts of life and behavior. The Center and Body feelings are ignored. It's like you are the horse pushing the cart—not making much headway and becoming exhausted. That is all reversed with LIFT: first you harness your child's feelings, the energy source of behavior, and then you are able to move forward a lot easier with establishing good behavior. If it sounds complicated, it's not. When you read Becky's inside story in Chapter 2, LIFT will become clear.

Emotions Run Everything

There are five basic emotions identified by science: Fear, Anger, Joy, Disgust, and Sadness. LIFT has customized this list based upon 50-plus years of counseling. Love has been substituted for Joy, and Disgust has been dropped. I've found Fear and Love are the primary emotions of humans. Fear is unpacked intrauterine, and Love requires unpackaging—this book does that for you. Anger is the energy and action source for Fear's possible fight, freeze, or flight actions. Kindness is Love's energy and action source.

Image this scene. Liam is yelling, "You never believe me!" And you know he didn't brush his teeth.

Here is the instinctual cart before the horse parenting: "I know you didn't brush your teeth. The toothbrush isn't even wet." And that's not the end of the arguing.

Inside Liam is fearful of your anger and counters it with his own anger. This cart-first focus is on his outside behavior, words and logic.

The LIFT approach places the horse before the cart as it should be—feelings before behavior. Your kind calm voice and body language harness Liam's feelings. Now you are in the sweet spot for calm behavior change. "I can tell you are really angry. Tell me more and I'll repeat what you say so you're sure I've heard you." This is how simple the starting point is for every conflict. The rest of the book will show you what to do after this starting point.

The Feelings-to-Behavior Cycle

There is a common cycle from our feelings to our behavior when something negative happens, either outside or inside. In nanoseconds the body responds in this order:

- Body sensations (one or a combination of the five senses felt)

- Emotions (in this case it's Fear) activated by the Mind in concert with the body

- Images are formed

- Thoughts try to make sense of the images, body sensations and emotions being felt

- Fight, freeze, or flight choices available

- Behavior happens—avoiding (flight), do nothing (freeze), or approaching (fight)

Why are emotions so central? They define two things about what happened: Value (how positive or negative the event was) and Intensity (how big a deal it was). Someone accidentally stepping on my toe? It's barely negative and no biggie—low value, low anger intensity. Simply saying "It's okay" to the other person marks the end. A car cutting me off? That can be big time negative and super big—high negative value, and high intensity anger. It could cause yelling, confrontation, and a lot of angry words. In short, emotions are the major contributor to our thoughts and resulting actions.

Let's put the LIFT stethoscope on and listen to Liam's inside cycle from emotions to behavior and hear the level of negativity and intensity.

"Mom's mad at me, my body's so tense, I'm scared, I've messed up again, I'm so stupid, I'm too scared to tell the truth, she'll really be mad and it doesn't matter that she said a thousand times 'if you just tell the truth we'll learn to trust you.'"

Have you ever wondered why your reasoning with someone like Liam never works? When his negative emotions build up and the intensity reaches a certain level, thinking and reasoning go out the window. A critical LIFT tool is to stop talking and get away from each other when these levels are reached.

Hopefully you are not feeling too discouraged or overwhelmed. Hear this loud and clear—you qualify for hope; everyone devoting the time to apply this information has bucket loads of love for their child. The lids stay on the buckets when we focus on behavior. With LIFT, you switch to the emotion channel, the lids fly off, and your child is filled with your love. In addition, fear's feeling of aloneness is gone, replaced by kindness and togetherness—the world we were intended to live in. And here is the most significant result: your child establishes the most basic human belief—I'm lovable. I can't wait for you to see right in front of your eyes how it unfolds and becomes deeply established.

Let's look at a few more facts about unattended fear. Fear guarantees:

- Negativity: "Nothing will ever work out," and an exclusive focus on what's wrong

- Low self-worth: "I'm bad," "I'm stupid"

- Separation: "I don't belong," aloneness, no one cares, knows or understands me

As I am writing this, I'm full of sadness at how unattended fear is so debilitating.

Unattended Conflict Destructs, Common Ground Constructs

9/11. The Indonesian tsunami. Suicide was the second leading cause of death in young people, ages 10–23 in both tragedies (2017). What emotion do you think fuels this? Yes, it's unattended fear. Bottom line: fear is all about surviving death—predicted, actual, or "feels like," even if it's the letter I have not opened from the IRS. If 9/11 happens again, will I die? Will my loved ones die? Suicide death might feel better than the terror felt 24/7. I live with this possibility every day in my practice. When you are inside a child's heart wanting to kill themselves, you can feel the living hell of life. (2017, age 15-24: 5,079)

Everyone has memories of past frightening things they have felt and usually can still recall. A little 1st grade boy, red headed, and freckle faced—so cute, at least that was the comment from adults. But every day he was made fun of, laughed at, and called "carrot top" by the other kids. He didn't know it at the time but going to school was like fearing 9/11 every day. It didn't help that he had ADHD, the type that interrupted all the time. He was always able to make people laugh and got two "U"s (unsatisfactory) on his first report card: interrupting and talking too much. It never dawned on him that he could tell someone about his inside pain. As a matter of fact, he experimented with sandpaper to take the freckles off. That hurt too much!

Even though I went through two years of twice-a-week therapy in my early 30s, I can still feel in my gut at 76 years old the dull dread feeling, seeing the image of myself as this little 1st grader being teased. And even though it sounds funny, I can still see a carrot top image on the top of my head. That's how horrific the mind can be when fear is unattended. And I still have some residual "I'm bad" ground that I regularly cultivate with loving kindness to myself—

and it really works, well most of the time. Thank goodness for my grey hair and aging skin with hardly any freckles!

Every one of you have experiences of unattended fear—some stories sound worse than others. There are good fear stories, too: when you avoided something awful like a car accident or a bad business deal. That image is in 3D color—no glasses needed. The stories are the normal deep emotional inside fear of being disliked, inadequate, and alone, hardly ever reaching the level of words spoken out loud but churning around inside of you daily. So sad.

Yes, unattended fear is an unbelievably powerful, destructive energy, the fuel source for conflict. It can kill people and clearly dampens each person's potential.

But good news—I've found a renewable energy source that can take fear out of conflict. It is as common and powerful as the wind and sun. This source establishes "I'm loveable" identity through a core value of "I have good value." The renewable energy source is activated Love.

Lovability guarantees continued fulfillment of our fundamental need to belong. It is the sensation of oneness that is the most satisfying of all feelings. This need is as basic as food and shelter experienced in a variety of ways: connection, together, sameness, agreement. Loneliness is considered by some an epidemic in America. 54% of Americans in a recent Cigna survey said they always or sometimes feel that no one knows them well.

Love is the renewable energy source. It's there all the time with potential limitless energy—that's the good news. The bad news is most of us hardly ever get past its *kumbayah* good feeling on the receiving side, and rarely use its unlimited power during conflict.

Think and see a wind turbine and the resulting electricity that lights up your home. Now think and feel a love turbine that transforms fear's stormy winds into calmness, a sense of belonging and oneness. Can you hear the chorus, *You are my sunshine…*?

Here are the turbine's mechanical steps that simultaneously deflate fear (separating) and inflate belonging (oneness):

- Conflict is reframed as an okay difference

- Surface differences are acknowledged without shame

- Center feelings (body, emotions, and images) causing the differences are validated

- Center validation is a deep oneness sensation of "I'm valued"

- Solutions are created from the Center's oneness

- "I'm lovable" and "I love you" resonates from the center.

Here is the turbine in action

I can't tell you how many comments I got at my husband's party last night with my new, knock-out red sequined dress. And my husband whispered in my ear, "Let's call in the Vogue photographers." I didn't remember the next day was the end of the month and it was our budget meeting time. Oops! It's the last thing we both want to do, but I print out the color budget for the month and immediately we both focus on the big red $200 on the bottom line in dead silence—the exact cost of my dress, and this isn't my first rodeo with things like this. Then something happened completely unexpected. My husband gently reached over to hold my hand and smiling like he really meant it, said, "What was it like to buy that dress and wear it?"

I gathered up my courage and gingerly shared how fun it was, avoiding eye contact as much as possible. After we had fun talking about it, I agreed to come up with some new ways to get a handle on this stuff. You know, I fully expected a blowout. After it was over, I couldn't believe how close I felt to him and wondered if we could handle all our differences this way in the future.

The Egg Really Is the Starting Point

Now you know all the working parts of how the egg becomes a chicken and how to make the egg deliver the best chicken possible. Every end behavior starts at our deepest Center: body sensations, emotions, and images. Then our unattended, negative-oriented mind, fueled by fear, makes distorted sense out of it and delivers thoughts that turn into behavior. Debilitating conflict far too often is the outcome.

Unbundled love to the rescue. Fear's destructive divide and conquer is replaced with Love's constructive belonging and win/win. And the starting point is validation at one's feeling epicenter: body and emotions are the first feelings a person has, accompanied with images when something happens. Does it sound too good to be true? You will know it isn't after reading the next chapter about how a mom pulled it off with her difficult daughter, Becky.

CHAPTER 2

Accepting Emotions During Conflict? Everything Changes

Please don't get mad at my yelling and arguing.
I'm scared inside and need your kindness.

LET'S TUNE IN TO Becky's thoughts and find out what she learned about emotions and behavior:

I didn't know when I yelled or argued that I had emotions causing it all.

I got to the point of always yelling at mom when she told me to get off my computer and quit playing Fortnite. And it always happened when I was making the best move ever. I've never had so much fun!

Mom's face gets this super mean look and she yells at me about never obeying, and how the computer was ruining the family's life, and I just lose it—yelling and calling her names. After I finally get off the computer, I always lose my computer privileges for several days. I really feel bad for what I say and promise myself I won't do it next time, but the same thing happens over and over.

I really thought there was something wrong with me. And then mom doesn't talk with me for several hours afterwards. It felt like someone dumped me on a road, like people trying to get rid of a dog. It makes me scared (fear causes disconnect).

You know what? In the last Fortnite competition, I got first out of 200 players! For the first time in my life I really felt successful—well most of the time. There's no way I was going to give up playing Fortnite!

Then one day mom did the weirdest thing. She asked to talk with me. Her face was calm, and her voice was nice (love causes connection). She said, "I realized Fortnite is about the best thing that ever happened to you. Is that right? Tell me what you love about it."

I was thinking, "Weird! No one has ever asked me this question. Everyone's been so mad at me." Then I just told her what I liked and how I'm really good at it. What was crazy is she was smiling and nodding while I talked. I felt funny inside, almost a tickling feeling—hard to describe.

Then she said something even crazier. "Let's find a way you can play so we don't get mad and yell at each other. It's the anger that causes the yelling and arguing. Now I can see why you get so mad at me. I'd be mad, too. It would be like Dad stopping me from eating ice cream. That will never happen!

We both laughed. Mom does enjoy ice cream, especially cookies and cream. And that stuff about anger causing yelling kind of makes sense. Can't believe it's actually natural and not me being messed up. She said she'd like to watch me play. Now that was really weird.

Then she asked me what would work when it's time to stop the game. I finally came up with the idea of a timer set for ten minutes to turn off the computer. She agreed. And if I didn't quit after ten minutes, mom would turn off the computer and I couldn't use the computer for twenty-four hours.

Mom gave me a hug and left. I sat there feeling funny inside. Like how's it possible to talk with mom about Fortnite and I wasn't yelling and arguing? I didn't even know what it felt like. I'd never felt it before. No, I'll take that back. I felt it when everyone clapped at school when I got second place in the spelling bee. A good feeling—way better then yelling, which I just found out was from anger. That's normal? Whatever!

Later that day Mom did watch me play and asked me all kinds of questions. I felt funny inside again—didn't know what to say or do. Oh well. Then we did the new shutting off the computer thing in ten minutes. It was really hard to do, but it worked, and mom never had that angry face and no yelling, so that really helped. After a couple times it got easier, and we don't have a problem with it anymore.

Are you wondering how Mom could shift her approach so radically? Here's the inside story: all too often feeling like she is on trial. First, realizing to how awful every mom feels with constant failure: guilty until proven innocent. Second, accepting the verdict and submitting to mediation—therapy.

Presumed guilty until proven innocent? Becky's mom is just like everyone else. Who has time to search for that tangled LIFT stethoscope? It's really complicated sorting everything out. We all have about 40 unattended thoughts per minute that are fear-fueled and delivered through frustration or anger.

I just don't have time to listen and the mega horn is handy and always on. At that moment, it's a relief to hear my booming voice, but not afterwards. Besides, it's five minutes before dinner is served, my other child is complaining of an earache, and now the oven timer sounds off. Plus, I have a least an hour of work to do tonight for a big board meeting tomorrow. And I don't want to look upset when Mike comes through the door, again. And you talk about guilt—I'm starting to dread being around Becky. I feel like a complete failure as a parent; seems she's always angry at me. I read the other day how computer games can make kids more agitated. They must have been researching Becky. I'm so worried about her. Oh, there's Mike coming in the door, and off to my other side is Becky, still on the computer when I told her to shut it off. That's only sixteen thoughts at once.

Let me stop by the side of the road and give my therapist "mom testimony." The above is the little bit I know about moms, not being one myself. It's taken years to start to appreciate what moms do and who they are at the core of their hearts. My best teacher was one of the greatest moms ever—my wife, followed by my daughters, and over four thousand moms who have honored me by seeking my assistance as a therapist. Of all those precious moms, I've never known one that doesn't go to bed at night and get up in the morning without thinking about their kids. Needless to say, I hold moms in a very revered and sacred place.

Oh, and my own mom—how was it possible she could live a satisfying life into her nineties having raised four boys (and the red-headed one counted as two; he had and still has severe ADHD). Every Sunday after church I could count on my Sunday School teacher conferencing with my mom and dad. You think it might have been about my amazing spiritual insights? I wish. No, the inevitable question was, "Do you think you can help him not be such a clown?" (I shouldn't admit it but writing this made me chuckle.) Also, my mom told everybody I ran before I walked. You know, I never remember her giving me consequences for this stuff or making me feel too bad about myself. I sure got my share of mini lectures though. I knew instinctively where the mute button was.

Becky's mom is having the pretrial experience of every parent I've counseled for the last 50 years. This normal parenting stuff is always fueled by underlying fear and delivered with frustration and anger. You already know what it does—it violates the deepest rule of the heart, splitting two people apart during a difference. Divide and conquer is instinctual but deadly. Thank goodness there is Love.

So, let us submit to mediation and see if we can avoid the trial. Go ahead, find the stethoscope and put it into your ears. Listen carefully—it will pick up feelings and thoughts, too, even the ones that are unconscious. What's unbelievable is that your thoughts and comments will bypass the mind and come from your Center. At first, you'll hear an annoying ringing sound to answer the mind's thoughts. Just simply turn the switch from Mind to Center.

Mediation Verdict: Both semi-guilty and sentenced to inside/out LIFT parenting counseling. The following is from the mediation transcript—mom's thoughts and notes during counseling. Mom had already reviewed the therapist website and read the eight LIFT kid stories that explained his approach. She also sent him a complete deposition on Becky's thoughts and their exchanges.

I couldn't believe how flat out scared I was sitting across from someone I didn't even know. My month was as dry as a bone. It helped that he reminded me of my grandpa and his first question, although unexpected, really helped. "What would you like to know about me—anything goes." I for sure didn't want to spend bucks on his story. But it only took about five minutes and was interesting to hear his inside story. I did ask why he wasn't retired. He said with a chuckle. "I still have plenty of tread left and the ride is really great." He leaned forward just a little bit and with a quiet voice said: "I couldn't wait to meet you and see if anything I know will help with Becky." Oh, and it helped when he said the main thing he's learned parenting four kids and nine grandkids is humility.

Here are the main points that made sense to me.

- *Focus on inside positive feelings*: He told me Becky felt really happy, good about herself, and successful with Fortnite. Inside I bolted. I don't want her to be happy with Fortnite. But I forced myself to pull the ear plugs out. Focus on Becky's inside happy, good, and successful self as she plays Fortnite, not how much I despise Fortnite. All the healthy chemicals are flowing in the brain wiring system (serotonin, dopamine, oxytocin, and endorphins). Of course, we want these chemicals flowing for school, sibling relationships, and giving to others. And he said all this stuff was establishing deep down important beliefs, like "I'm good" and "I can count on myself." Weird, almost right away the fog was clearing. I'm a geological engineer. Most of the soil conditions under the surface are very different. Yes, of course I want her to feel good and be self-assured.

- *Fear's body language/images/feelings/thoughts/comments:* He explained Becky's and my yelling came from fear: Becky feared my rejection and loss of positive feelings (Fortnite), and I feared her lack of respect and becoming a gamer for life. He helped me realize the bottom line is that I was really scared of being a failure and he agreed with me if I did just surface studies in my work, the failure rate would be high. And talking about surface stuff, I didn't realize it but my angry body language—frowning, squinted eyes— was as scary as my loud voice. And the images—I don't want to think about that. I can still see my dad's angry face. The video clips played right away—yuck. And the words I used like "never" and "ruining our family" likely made Becky feel like Godzilla. In between these points he helped me with some breathing exercises to lessen the dentist-hitting-the-nerve type pain. He also said not speaking to her for two hours often feels like being put on life support. And all this fear pumps the stress hormone cortisol throughout the body, signaling fight, freeze, or flight. Now I could see where both of our anger was coming from.

I just never realized how all this underground fear and surface anger happens automatically. Right away I thought of the blowout yesterday in an oil field I was responsible for, and how we installed pressure-control systems and the flow was super productive. We both had a good laugh when the therapist said, "Now you can add 'anger blowout specialist' to you resume."

I must admit during the first part of the session when all the info was rolling out, I felt how a bull must feel in a china shop. How could I possibly not destroy everything when it is all so new, and each mistake would be so costly?

Also, more good news: he said with the LIFT pressure systems in place, the brain can be effectively re-wired, significantly reducing the old memories, minimizing cortisol flow and maximizing serotonin, oxytocin, endorphins and dopamine. These wires are call neuropathways. Their ability to be modified is now proven by advanced neuroimaging. I could feel a change in my body with the hope he was giving me. Pretty amazing; and the therapist's excitement at my receptiveness was really making me happy.

For the next 15 minutes, he gave me LIFT's quick start instructions.

LIFT'S L-O-V-E action steps: It's stethoscope time

The therapist gave me a white sheet of paper and ask me to write LOVE in big letters across the top of page. Then he asked, "What do you think would be a loving response when Becky yells at you about getting off the computer, one that would result in her stopping the yelling and obeying you?"

"Well… I could tell her she could play as long as she wanted. The yelling would certainly stop but she'd never stop playing."

The therapist leaned a bit forward in his chair. "Would she feel your love?"

"Of course, but I would never get paid back with respect. She'd never get off the computer. I've tried every reward in the books. And you already know—nothing works."

He chuckled, "Yeah, and that's what you're paying me the big bucks for. Okay, imagine a stethoscope, attach it to your ears, and move the end of it to Becky's heart, and away from her mouth. Oh, I forgot, in case you feel your bitten tongue will bleed, I've got gauze strips to put in you mouth. Now we are going to roleplay LOVE. Write down on the page from the letter L, Listen. It's a code word for No Talking.

Listen. I tell him what Becky says and how she acts (see above story). We then accessed the Center/feeling translator, putting everything into normal, Center, deep-down feeling language. I couldn't believe the number of times I needed to switch off my mind thinking "can you image a kid talking to a parent like that?" and zip the comments. He helped me translate everything into feelings: "You never let me have any fun" translated to "I'm fearful and angry that you won't allow something that's good in my life." After several minutes I started to get the hang of it. Actually, it was a relief. I'd never really done this deep stuff with myself and I could see how I also had a lot of feelings I had never realized. Now we moved on to the O in Love. I wrote Observe.

Observe. This is repeating only what you *saw* and *heard* from Becky's center. Even after practicing, it was still hard for me to not slam down my two dollars' worth, and keep my calm, kind mask from falling off. My observed points are followed by, "Did I get it?" "Yes" is the requirement before moving on to the Validating step. I wrote down Validate.

Validate. Three parts: Repeating (done in the Observe step), Agreeing, and Empathizing. The therapist made several points. Conflict is dead on arrival with agreeing and empathizing. If you disagree with everything, you can always agree with an emotion, "That makes sense to me how mad you'd be." And empathizing puts the icing on the cake, without carbs or calories. "I'd be mad if I were you."

Becky can be deadly. "You're the worst mom ever." Before this session, hell would need to freeze over before I agreed with that one. But when the therapist reminded me of how I installed the pressure control system on that well blowout, I could see and feel the possibility of us agreeing. The deadly comment was a blowout fueled by fear and anger. I could look deeper at the anger pressure source and agree with it. It's about knowing how all the underlying pieces work and avoiding the surface debris.

Looking underneath the "worst mom ever" comment helped me see it was her deep-down disappointment and disconnection that caused the surface angry statement. After several touch-and-goes,

I got the agreement and empathy comment out. "I agree with your anger when the best thing ever is Fortnite and I tell you to stop." And the empathy. "It'd be like me going to my ice cream shop, the server dipping a sample spoon into the cookies and cream, putting the spoon right to my mouth, then you say, 'no way.' Now that's a china shop demolished in seconds and I'd get to the ice cream no matter what."

I had to say it out loud several times before I could image pulling this stuff off. Then he pointed out how being at this deepest level of a person when tornados are flying above is one of the most permanent love experiences for Becky: "Now I'm understood when I'm bad," "the deepest parts of me are normal when I fail, am wrong, or make someone mad." He pointed out something cool about the word understand: always look *under* where you *stand*.

You know what was really strange during the last part of this discussion? I could feel the attachment chemicals flowing—dopamine, oxytocin, endorphins, and serotonin. Cortisol was dead in the water. I didn't realize it, but the therapist said this validating part is the heart of developing bedrock self-confidence fueled by parent certifying "I'm lovable" for children. And apparently "I'm lovable" is the endless source of true happiness. I'll need to think about that for a while.

Then he asked me to write Evoking beside the E, which is the mutual problem-solving step.

Evoking. Mutual solution from the Center (Center deep diving for mutual solutions). The therapist said there are three steps, each requiring Becky's buy-in.: (1) parameters, (2) choice, (3) follow-through consequences. To set parameters, I need to decide the maximum Fortnite playing time and a set time range to choose from—for example 1 hour, maybe between 6 and 8 PM. Parameters need to be within a range Becky and I could both accept. He said this is Center planning—each knowing the other's feelings and demonstrating respect through open discussion and mutual solutions.

Here are several consequence guidelines he gave me. Big picture: make sure the plan will be ninety-nine percent successful. And there are some specific guidelines. Rewards can be used, but for this situation, take-aways were recommended for maximum motivation. First, make the consequence just long enough to get Becky's attention—not fueled solely by a parent's frustration. Also, consequence shelf-life is short—too long and they lose their energy. If a child uses something daily, the first consequence attempt usually is one day. Determine KIS (keep it simple) rules. Make things too complicated and we enter into a presidential debate. Time to get off the computer is the target with a timer being the referee. Again, give your time range from which Becky can choose. Then ask for her input about consequences. Caution: Don't use this tactic if you are sure her consequence will not be acceptable. Otherwise, simply inform her about your consequence. Consequences are only as good as your policing and follow through.

As he walked me through the consequence info, I realized these buy-in, mutuality, 99% successful plan points were all standard procedure at my job. From this bottom-up approach, it's so obvious how respect for the other person's Center pays huge dividends for everyone. And I'm now sold on my stethoscope. Oh, my tongue is completely healed. And I must tell you, looking back on the old way I handled this feels like the wheel had not been invented.

Lesson Learned

Smooth sailing can be expected when emotions are your steady-as-she-goes rudder.

CHAPTER 3

Love Infused Conflict =
Self-Confidence

*Stop how scared I am about failure
so I can feel okay about myself.*

SEVEN-YEAR-OLD ADALEE says, "Mistakes help me learn. I know I can do this."

Can a seven-year-old really experience that much self-confidence? Yes, it's a true story but it's a rare exception. Good news: LIFT has uncovered two secrets to self-confidence.

The First Secret

**Fear of failure, found within every daily conflict,
erodes self-confidence.**

A parent's response to failure requires extreme caution. Fear's immediate fight or flight instinct needs to be stopped dead in its tracks.

Adalee didn't always think mistakes were for learning. It seemed to all start by the second semester of first grade; Adalee remembered feeling discouraged about school.

Every day she heard, "Adalee, let's take more time with your writing." And at home Dad was frustrated: "We've been over this spelling list enough times for you to get them right this time." But reading to mom was the worst: "I know you know these words. You are so smart. It shouldn't take you this long to read three pages."

Adalee shared with me:

Many sad and angry self-thoughts started popping up a lot by the beginning of second grade. And almost every time I felt a burning feeling in my stomach, and other times I felt cold inside. I'm kind of scared to go home and go to school. It's like I'm always doing something wrong. All the other kids write and read better than me. And some of them tease me about it.

Why can't I try hard enough? That's what my teacher and parents say I need to do. I used to think I was trying really hard and I kept telling Mom and Dad that, but they didn't believe me. I've given up saying anything. I believe everyone and I know I'm a person that can't try hard enough.

I am happy about one thing—Fluffy, my very own cat. I love the way she cuddles up to me and purrs. I feel so warm and cozy. Funny, sometimes I wish I could take her to school with me.

Now I'm sure about two things: It's all my fault and I know why I'm really messed up. I've got to be a bad person for making everyone mad at me. It's got to be true. No one is happy with me.

It's so sad what can happen down deep inside a child when outside failure is the sole focus. Unbridled fear is off to the races: it's always negative, the body tightens up, it's always "all my fault," and ends up with "I'm bad." At least that's what I've witnessed in my practice with every one of the over four-thousand children who have opened up their hearts. Every time it eventually comes out with tears and my heart breaks like the first time I heard it.

But good news—that's were the second secret comes in.

The Second Secret

Make sure a child *feels* "I have value" and "I'm lovable" at *the beginning* of a failure.

Adalee is now in the last semester of the second grade, feeling worse than ever. Let's check in with her during one of her monthly "feelings" classes—this one about sadness.

The counselor responded to Adalee's raised hand. "I think I'm sad a lot, can I …" Through the tears and the counselor placing a hand on her shoulder, she finished, "Can I talk with you alone?" Handing her a tissue the counselor said softly, "We'll do it today in my office." And then she addressed the class with most kids' faces looking down at their desks, "I'm so proud of Adalee for sharing her inside feelings," Then she looked at Adalee, " Joy from the movie *Inside Out* would really be proud of you." Adalee brushed a tear away, "Oh, Joy, I really like her."

Later that day Adalee shared everything with her counselor. All kinds of thoughts rushed through her mind after hearing the counselor explain the possible reasons for her school problems. "So, there's another reason for my problems? It's a different way I learn? Some weird word that sounds like the Alexa thing we have at home—something like 'dyslexia.'"

Anyway, what my counselor explained is exactly what happens to me when I have trouble reading and writing. She said it's normal for the stomach to feel upset and have other feelings like sadness, maybe anger, or disappointment about always being told how wrong I was. I guess my feelings and body got tangled up together and a person can feel physically upset when you really are not sick. And she said it had nothing to do with me down deep inside. She reminded me of the caregiver of the month award I got last month and that I am a wonderful girl that reads and spells differently. And the best thing she said is that she knows how to fix school so people accept the way I learn. That can't be true.

Fast forward past the Dyslexia testing Adalee received and LIFT counseling. Let's tune in to Adalee just starting her the last quarter of the second grade.

I can't believe how easy school is. The teachers now give me reading and writing assignments that I get 80s and 90s on. And homework, well mom and dad are doing the same thing, giving me stuff that makes me feel good. Now I'm getting that Fluffy feeling most of the time at school and home. I'm so happy.

Oh, and another thing, the counseling really helped. Here's what happened almost right away. With the LIFT counselor's help, Mom and Dad said the same thing she did with a lot of tears, "We are so sorry for being angry at you for something you could not help. We promise from now on we'll listen carefully to your deep-down feelings about everything." Now that was worth three Fluffys. I started crying and jumped out of my chair for a group hug. The therapist stepped out for a minute so we could take all the time we needed. It was so good to feel together about something that always felt wrong and bad before.

We learned a lot of good stuff, but the best was how to do mistakes. The therapist explained any time there's a problem, our brain pops into survival mode—like what's wrong, what horrible thing is going to happen, stuff like that. Almost the same feeling I had when I was in a car accident with my parents. I was OK, but for the first minute I thought maybe I was going to die. The counselor helped mom and dad know that in the past, I felt a lot of these scared feelings. And mom and dad believed him—I felt so relieved.

Anyway, the therapist said when a mistake happens, expect to be scared. It's just normal and expect your body may feel tight and maybe ache. He said most of the time this fear is exaggerated, like at school yesterday when the fire alarm went off and it was only something wrong with the alarm. He did say to try to stop these body alarms right away. The breathing exercises he taught us are the first thing to do when we feel the body alarms. It's weird when you pay attention to the emotional and body signals with the breathing; feels like the fear flames are doused. My stomach burning hardly ever happened again. Yay!

So, with mistakes, he taught mom and dad to stay calm, ask about, and agree with my feelings. Then all we needed to come up with were ideas to decrease the chance of mistakes the next time. After each session we practiced it a lot together. And yeah, we had way more Fluffys than ever. I still don't know how it can feel good even when I mess up, but it does.

Important Points:

Unattended Mind Processing Unit (UMPU) vs Center Processing Unit (CPU)

A computer's basic job is to process information from keyboard entry to resulting information on the screen. So far, we have witnessed how focusing on a behavior uses the fear-based UMPU, and LIFT uses the Love-based CPU.

Let's summarize what we've learned so far about the necessity of switching on LIFT's CPU when failure starts.

- Inside body feelings and emotions are the start of everything.

- Unattended activated Fear kick starts everything. UMPU's negative bias processes outside failure, resulting in negative feelings—body and emotions: cold, tightness, separation, feeling unliked, misunderstanding, and some form of "I'm bad."

- Activating LOVE's (CPU) positive bias will process failure inside, through oneness. Feelings include warmth, relaxation, togetherness, being liked, understood, and some form of "I'm okay." Conflict is transformed from splitting/destruction to joining/construction, ending in satisfying behavior change.

- Deepest self "I" is separated from outside failure—feels safe, secure, and self-assured.

- Outside failure is processed as "I like learning so I can be a better person."

- "I have good value" and know "I am lovable" are continually reinforced.

Bottom line: Unattended fear destructs; activated LOVE constructs.

Value: "I am liked" (I am lovable).

Failure is the epicenter of value creation and maintenance

There are two parts of an underground earthquake: the focus point or earthquake's beginning, and the surface epicenter located directly above the focus. When buildings and their foundations are built to withstand the epicenter shaking, very little damage occurs. That's what happened in Alaska's 2018 7.1 earthquake. There was limited damage and no deaths.

Adalee's first year in school was an earthquake of sorts that diminished her deep-down value, leaving her feeling like "it's all my fault and I'm messed up and bad." After several LIFT counseling sessions, here is what Dad and Mom made out of the initial earth-shattering experience.

"I had no idea what impact I had on Adalee by continually asking her to try harder." Mom bushed a tear away and continued, "You and I, along with a lot of other people, always said what a bright girl she was. I still can't believe how many times I repeated this and completely missed feeling her pain."

Dad reached out to hold her hand, "I know, I did the same thing and what I really feel bad about is my short fuse. I really didn't notice Adalee's fear of my anger. I had no idea, but I can see it now, that she's an empath. And you said your counselor helped you to see you're one too?"

(Mom started counseling after they went into LIFT family counseling with Adalee.) "Yeah, I kind of knew it but I really tried to shove it down because in my early school days, I'd cry at the drop of a hat. I got teased a lot and my mom and dad said I'd better get a stiff upper lip, or I'd never make it in adult life. I was successful and voila, stuffing it down turned into depression and blinders.

"And one of the craziest revelations, thank goodness, was that Adelee's sensitivity triggered the fear in my buried emotions, and I dealt with it indirectly by insisting she just try harder." After a couple deep breaths, she continued, "I just had no idea about what humans are like, you know, how the therapist said most of who we are is unconscious."

"Yes, I agree," Dad nodded. "I admire your courage in uncovering all this stuff in counseling. I'm not looking forward to doing my own digging in my first session next week. What I can't get over is how we all have two worlds: the outside and inside. I kind of always knew it, but really didn't grasp it. The biggest thing I didn't get was the run-away train effect of fear when failure happens.

"Until now I could not understand how five years later, I still feel bad about myself when I didn't pass my bar exam the first time. When Adalee told us in our sessions the stuff she felt secretly, like not feeling any good within her, you didn't know it, but I could hardly stay in the room because it's what I still say to myself." For the first time in years, tears were falling down his cheek and he continued, "I'm sorry," he looks at this wife. "I'm learning this inside stuff is normal, but man it feels so embarrassing to even talk about it with anyone. Anyway, I'm really relieved we are truly getting to the bottom of stuff."

Mom's been holding his hand and with her empath voice says, "Oh, what I would have given to have a Dad like you." They hug and both feel the Fluffy chemicals flow through their bodies.

Mom and Dad's take away:

Becoming one (joining) with deep-down emotions creates value and diminishes fear of surface failure.

CHAPTER 4

Avert an 8.5 Earthquake When Your Child Makes a Mistake

Know your upset makes me feel scared,
like you'll never love me.

I ALMOST ALWAYS CRY when I make a mistake. Come on—I'm ten. I get so angry at myself. My mom and dad are getting really frustrated with me, too. I can't stop saying the same old thing: "What's wrong with me? I'm so stupid," and stuff like that. I finally went to the school counselor. She sent me to our earth science teacher who teaches a new eighth grade class called Earth/Human Science. What I learned changed everything.

The first thing he said is that our earth has lessons to teach us. Whatever! That sounded crazy to me, but I keep my mouth shut.

Then he put up this diagram called "Mind Earthquake and the Fear Fault Line." It showed a fault line cracking open into two parts, like when there is an earthquake. And from the breaking point (Focus Point), seismic anger waves radiated to the surface (Epicenter) where everything was a mess. He had pictures of kids banging their heads and parents yelling at kids and everything around them was broken. Two days ago, I barely survived an Alaska earthquake. It was really scary—I mean really, really scary!

Then he told us something like an earthquake happens inside us when we mess up. He said all of us have a Fear Fault Line, and it splits apart when we make a mistake. Everything feels tight like someone has a grip on you and is shaking you. He pointed to the anger waves coming out of the Center Focus Point and said anger is released from us and from adults. The worst part is self-directed anger. Just like in an earthquake, the anger eventually goes away, but not the thoughts and feelings. I couldn't believe what I was hearing—that was me! I looked around the class and almost everyone else was nodding their heads in agreement.

He was right. When I make a mistake, down deep inside me I feel the same fear as I had during the earthquake: Something's wrong. My body gets super tight and tense. Will I die? There's no way to stop this. I'm finished! Then I started to cry—so embarrassing—but was able to stop.

I pointed to the anger waves coming from the Focus Point. "What's this?"

"Well, when we're fearful, anger kicks in to fight or flight," he explained. "That's the mind's way of trying to get rid of the outside threat. In this case, it's making a mistake. We get mad at ourselves, feeling like, 'I'm dumb,' and parents can get mad, too, yelling things like, 'When will you ever learn?'"

Then he had some good news. This mind earthquake eventually gets over the mistake. But the two-part bad news is this: we feel completely alone and misunderstood by our parents, and we feel something is basically wrong down in our Center. ("I'm wrong, not just my behavior.") This "I'm wrong" feeling, along with way-down inside tenseness, usually stays long after the earthquake is over—Yuck!

Barely able to hold back the tears—again—I nodded in agreement and told him, "That's exactly what I feel like. How do I fix it?" My body felt a mix of tense and relaxed—weird.

"There's a new fix called LIFT," he told me. "The minute a mistake happens, parents learn to do something completely different. They switch their attention to the inside starting, Focus Point of the earthquake. They don't talk about all the stuff happening at the epicenter surface. A parent's anger, making you feel like you are unloved, is replaced with understanding kindness, and that funny feeling of a grip on you is released.

"It sounds crazy, but using LIFT is like spraying a gigantic fire hose on the flaming fear. It reduces it to just a little smoke. It's normal to be scared when a mistake happens, and the mind tries to get rid of the fear with anger. LIFT is very effective. The cool part is that when fear is reduced to a little smoke, almost all the anger goes away, too, and you have a chance to see what's OK about you. You can breathe a lot easier."

I'm feeling warmth in my body, just a little, as I imagine this happening—really strange. I blurt out, "Do parents like this really exist, and how is it possible to not be angry at myself?"

"I agree it sounds crazy but here's the deal. The mind earthquake causes animal-like things to happen—threat happens, the fearful fight or flight is turned on, all the muscles get tensed for action. We are fueled by anger and we don't even know it's happening. At the deep, inside Focus Point we experience—feel, not know—all of this as 'we are going to die.' It almost always starts out as an 8.5 Richter scale earthquake with a lot of inside confidence damage and a feeling of being separated from your parent. The biggest part is feeling misunderstood and alone," my teacher explained. Now I can see why I cry so easily, just like I did during the Alaska earthquake.

"This animal response works OK when your dad swerves to miss a car crash, but it's worse than useless when you need to deal with your parent's anger at getting an F in Math."

He pulls out another diagram called "Center Earthquake." He points to the Center (earthquake's Focus Point) showing a kid being gently touched on his shoulder by a parent. With a kind face, they are saying, "You feel scared and angry but that will go away as we support you to find different ways to think and feel when a mistake happens." It's funny, but I can feel the gigantic fire hose right at my center. The diagram shows the two parts of the fault line merged and eventually completely reconnected with two very light anger waves going out to the surface, instead of ten. Whew! Now my body feels warm like the coziest blanket ever.

He explained that when parents do this every time, eventually there is little to no anger at yourself, and mistakes are processed as easily as knowing when you get hungry, you can eat and feel better. I must be dreaming! Is this possible? The parent's input requires constant kindness, just like a healthy body requires daily fruits and vegetables. Regular anger is as unhealthy as constantly eating French fries and hamburgers—yum. Anger causes mind earthquakes to happen way too much. Starting everything at the Center keeps things intact at the surface epicenter.

I point to the merged fault line, "Does this stay permanently united?"

I learned the fault line will remain strong, even though there will be an occasional hairline fracture because of life's ups and downs. Repeated, kind attachment at the starting point strengthens the Fear Fault Line and makes it stronger and stronger. The scary feeling of separation from parents is gone. When they agree with your first feelings—now that's understanding. Your Center experiences joining, calm, and valued: "I'm OK, even though I messed up." "Wrong" is only distant lightning on the horizon. And the really good news: The Fear Fault Line is actually strengthened with each healing experience. "I'm lovable" is the inevitable resulting belief.

I really felt hopeful for the first time. "Will you call my parents and let them know how to learn this stuff?"

Important points:

First let's pop the hood and take a brief tour of the fear mechanics operated by the two human CPU Operating Systems: UMOS (Unattended Mind Operating System) and COS (Center Operating system).

Fear Fault Line: UMOS, operates unconsciously

1. Fear is the body's first response to threat. Fear is one with the body (embodied). Feelings start everything. Thoughts are second. The Fear experience shuts off our good bias Center. It is still connected but switched off.

2. Fear's instinctive, felt threat response: survive impending death. Cortisol (threat hormone) flows throughout the body and simultaneously the Mind determines the best fight or flight plan, all initially happening outside our awareness. Then it's all-hands-on-deck; the plan goes live with 3D feelings, thoughts, and action steps.

3. Fear's *beginning* felt response cannot distinguish between an aggravating gnat and a car pulling out in front of you. All initial threat, whether emotional or physical, is experienced (felt) as physical impending death, whether you are being yelled at or your finger is smashed.

4. Fear and Mind always complete the survival drill. It's over but results are horrible. The information is stored in our data bank (science label—somatic marker) for future reference.

5. Mind's data bank references are created from a negative bias: 40 thoughts a minute, two out of three are negative. All thoughts are distorted but they are stimulated by real situations.

6. **Mechanics UMOS Summary:** *Unconscious threat processes work great for physical danger but are overkill for emotional danger. New OS is required.*

LIFT's Center Operating System: COS, consciously reducing Fear to "Danger Severity Signal" only.

1. Emotional threat component is added to the Fear processor, enabling both physical and emotional threats to be processed.

2. Center's LOVE (Listening, Observing, Validating, Evoking) good bias component processes Fear at the *beginning* of the threat, at the Focus Point. Parent/child validation attachment is forged, replacing angry separation. The immediate result is the Danger Severity Signal being activated and the Impending Death Signal being switched off. Immediately the body and emotional feelings are normalized through validation, threat solutions are mutually created and maintained, and downgraded destructive fear remains grounded in the Unattended Mind museum. LIFT's process changes the result to "I have value" and this eventually becomes the permanent living fuel. "I'm lovable" emerges as your child's core intended identity.

3. The child's "who I am" identity formulator component is continually activated, implementing normal human development principles. From birth, children are like sponges absorbing the parent's reflections, and that becomes who they are. LIFT's COS shuts off a parent's instinctual "mini me" projector and illuminates "who I am." LIFT parents constantly reflect the developing *child's* characteristics, always focusing on what's right and good. "You're wrong" is transformed into "an opportunity for improvement." Parents carefully monitor the "right" and "improvement" daily interactions to achieve at least 75%+ "right" to 25% "improvement" ratio. The body and emotion validations are always the first focus. LIFT's effective gigantic fire hose is always extinguishing unnecessary fear.

4. **Mechanics COS Summary: *Instinctive Fear is replaced by LOVE at the beginning of a threat, delivering constructive threat safety. Since "I am OK" with threat, confidence at a child's core is increasingly a done deal, and dreaded vulnera-***

bility no longer rules. The result is a child's assurance that "I have fundamental value" and "I'm lovable."

How To:

"Lucas, how many times have I told you to share your Lego bin with your …"

He stiffens and yells, "Mom, he's supposed to ask to play with it! He never does, and you always believe him. Why aren't you like dad? When I'm at his house, he always gets on Logan."

Mom frowns, shakes her head, grits her teeth and says, "Logan says he asks, and you always refuse. Anyway, you get another day off your phone for hitting him."

As mom walks away, Lucas runs in front of her walking backwards, "That's no fair! You never take things away from Logan."

Mom finally gets away and Lucas is left alone. Just then Patch comes running up to him. He picks her up to cuddle in his bed and she starts purring. But then the same old thoughts start racing in his mind and tears start dripping down his cheeks.

It is true what mom says. A lot of times Logan does ask me, but I always say no. Why can't I be a better brother? I really don't like Logan. I should like him. Sometimes when I see him, I get so mad. I try to keep it in. Everyone is always on his side saying stuff like, "He's your little brother, so you'll need to be more patient with him." The other thing—he never gets mad and is always doing everything mom and dad ask him to do, even extra things. That look on mom's face and how she hugs him every time he does the good stuff just feels like when my fishing line gets all tangled and I pull on one end and it gets tangled tighter.

He pounds the bed and there are more tears. He whispers as loud as he can, "I wish he was never born!" Patch is cowering in the corner now and Lucas coaxes her back beside him. He feels more distant than ever from Logan, Mom, and Dad. He falls asleep thinking, "I don't deserve to be liked. I better get used to being alone."

Then the family started attending LIFT sessions. After several sessions on the Focal Point information, Lucas tells me what happens to him underground daily, things never revealed to his parents. During the first several sessions, over three-fourths of the kids I counsel are not aware of their detailed feelings. But with the ongoing therapeutic warmth and validation, the darkness gradually lifts, and words are attached to those scary, emerging feelings. The length of time is usually longer with most teens. The darkness is caused by focusing on the epicenter outside behavior.

Once the darkness has mostly cleared, it's time for a Mom and Lucas session. Following each short vignette will be a brief explanation so you can apply the material. Don't get too discouraged about how stuck you are. Almost all parents get stuck—the same behaviors, same parent responses, same kid behaviors—everything cemented into place more and more.

Mom comes in first and sits on the right side of the couch, Lucas sits on the far-left side, almost on the arm rest. Mom's been prepped to listen, not interrupt, always stick to Lucas's point, and accept my coaching. The focus is changing from Lucas's "wrong perception" or "I understand," to validating his emotion." Skip saying, "I understand" or "that's your perception." Almost all kids do not believe you.

One of the main purposes of LIFT therapy is to train parents to be the therapist—who wants to be spending big bucks on therapy for many months? Here's a Focus Point summary of the deep-down issues. You will notice I often use "should" in the below bullet points. I'm acknowledging the beginning feelings (Focal Point) of his instinctual feelings, not trying to use logic. Logic never works at the beginning of a problem unless you want an argument.

- Lucas feels Mom loves Logan more than him. (Mom *is* nicer to Logan. I know, there's every reason to.)

- Mom does not trust Lucas. (Mom should not. Lucas lies a lot.)

- Lucas hates his bother. (Intense feelings of rejection from parents make hate a common feeling.)

- Lucas is jealous of Logan's non-angry temperament. (He should be. His opposite temperament is unlikable.)

- At his core, Lucas feels bad and like he doesn't belong—a central requirement. (He should. He does "bad" things all the time.)

- Lucas is a candidate for addictions, depression, and anxiety. (Pleasure is a fundamental need and will be searched for in any way possible.)

I look at Lucas. "Lucas, tell Mom how you feel about Logan."

Lucas squirms, looks at me, and then darts a quick glance at Mom who is tilting her head with a pleasant, sincere smile. "Mom, you don't do anything about Logan coming into my room and playing with my stuff."

Mom looks at me, back at Lucas, and then to me with a pleading look. So, I say, "OK, ask him to tell you more."

Lucas then gives her a lot of details and Mom does not interrupt, even though I counted five times she felt like it and said nothing.

"Mom, you really did a good job listening. Now without giving your point of view, tell Lucas what you heard him say." (This is the Observation and Validation part of the LOVE process.) Now Mom is right at the Focal Point and starting the mending process of the split Fear Fault Line.

Mom starts, "You said he always comes into your room without asking and then starts to play with your stuff even when you are not there. But…"

I wave my hand low and gently, "Mom, not now, later. Just keep telling him what you heard him say."

Lucas is darting looks at each of us as we exchange comments and is now leaning forward, really getting into it.

Mom continues looking at me, takes a deep breath and then kindly tells Lucas exactly what he had said. Lucas is nodding his head in agreement and a slight smile can be detected on his face. I say to Mom, "Ask him if that's what he said."

Lucas answers her as tears start welling up in his eyes, "Yes, and you—you always take his side."

Mom straightens, frowns, looks at him with the saddest expression and then quietly says to me, "Help me. I know I'll say the wrong thing." Wow, what a loving response.

"Say something like this: That's got to be a terrible feeling. I want to listen so I can know how awful that is for you and so I can change."

She says it beautifully while dabbing the tears off her cheeks. And he responds by going into more detail. Then, with some coaching, she responds. "You are right. I can see that I am nicer to Logan. I'd be hurt just like you are."

Here are the practical action steps to correct Lucas's belief that Mom likes Logan more than him.

- Every other weekend set aside a two-hour weekend time away from home doing what Lucas likes.

- Two, 15-minute fun times together Monday through Thursday.

- Enforcing Logan staying out of his room.

- Promising to listen carefully to his feelings about conflicts with Logan.

Summary:

Joining completely with the deep-down Focus Point feelings is a mending oneness feeling. No more earthquakes, and behavior always improves.

CHAPTER 5

Your Child's Fear:
Deflate Permanently to Live Fully

*Tell me calmly you feel the same emotions as me
during problems. This closeness makes me feel strong.*

"YOUR PSYCH PROFESSOR TALKING about forging a bond with parents at the deepest level, as early as possible, reminds me as a kid watching our town blacksmith firing up his forge with hot coal. One time he formed a hitch for my dad. As it got red hot, he hammered it into the shape Dad wanted."

Sarah was back home for Christmas break and telling her parents about one of her freshman year psychology classes: Deflating Abandonment Instinct—A Child's Greatest Fear.

Their eyes met and twinkled. "Dad, now I know what a forge is. I just love your stories."

She leaned forward, catching both Mom and Dad's eyes, and with a deep breath said, "Here's what else I learned. The prof said a kid's most unconscious, scary fear from birth is abandonment. They don't know it, but it feels like possible death. Upsetting differences with parents are the hottest, gut-wrenching times for a child. The big problem is feeling split apart. The child feels separated from parents and inside they feel like they are split between a lot of 'I'm bad' and very little 'I'm good.'

"Then he told us about a new way to forge everything together that deflates abandonment fear. The best time for forging is during the scariest times. The bonding starts by parents welding the split differences, and then forging a strong, permanent bond. "Mom, I couldn't wait to ask you about how welding works, since you did some welding as a teenager."

Sarah's Mom chimed in. "I'm so excited about what you're learning. Maybe you can present this to the suicide prevention group I head up. Anyway, my Dad helped me to be a welder on our Kansas farm. It's called stick welding. You have two pieces of metal you want to join. In one hand you have a torch and in the other a special metal rod. The tip of the rod melts between the metal pieces made hot by the torch, forging them together. I guess in your example the parents are responsible for the welding and the bonding?"

Almost interrupting she says, "You've got it, Mom. I'll get to that in just a minute. First a little 101 on inside and outside parts," Sarah continued. "The prof said there are two major parts of us. The deep-down affective, or feeling part, starting with body sensations, and coupled with our four basic emotions, the biggest ones being fear and love—the two others are sadness and anger. He said most people in Western society don't pay attention to them. Eastern religions have known this for over 4000 years. And then there's the more surface cognitive, thinking, and behavior part of us, which is more obvious.

"But here's the really cool new information. Abandonment fear usually gets worse when parents weld and forge at the surface level—you know, lectures and consequences about behavior. Things usually split open again because it's only welded on the surface. And there usually is no bonding, just anger and feeling scared."

Mom said, "This is interesting. It fits with what one of our consultants said—that at the deepest level, we all crave being the same. No one wants to be alone or split apart. If only your Dad liked jazz as much as I do. Dad shook his head with a forced smile. He also told us maybe this abandonment death fear is trauma from the umbilical cord being cut. Anyway, how do you weld and forge during scary differences?"

Sarah explained, "Well, it goes against our natural reaction, but it's actually easy and takes only three weeks of practice. There are three steps. During a conflict there is plenty of heat for welding. First the parent shuts off anger and validates the child's body sensations and emotions that are at the deepest part of a child. Then this causes the child to feel safe, even though things seem horrible, because the parent confirmed it and their calm validating words and actions are proof that there is nothing to fear. Finally, the biggest part is the child feels deep-down good with no bad feelings.

"Oh, by the way, the new theory establishes body sensations and emotions as the cause of thoughts and the resulting surface behavior. The welding rod is the parent calmly validating the deepest part of a child, first their body sensations and then their emotions. Like saying it's all right to feel shocking sensations and to be scared. It's normal, and no matter what, we are always here for you. You can always feel some good, even in the roughest times. And here's another part—apparently every child has a special Dad and Mom emotion validation receptacle in their most core being. If that validation from Dad and Mom is regularly plugged in exactly right, safety and good are assured during both smooth and rough times. Plug in the parents' validation enough times, or every time, and soon the abandonment fear is permanently deflated. No more splitting. The inside and outside bonding is permanently forged.

"And mom, your consultant was right about sameness. That craving for sameness he mentioned is established permanently during the scary situation. Mom, Dad, and child feel the same emotions, all is safe, and everyone feels they are good. After enough repetition, the child feels the permanent presence of a validating parent. The feeling of 'I'm good and safe' is welded into place. The prof said it's called object permanency. I guess a lot of books have been written on the subject.

"Oh, and here's the big win," Sarah finished with a smile. "It all ends with a child's most critical human identity being established—I'm lovable. And the big bonus, the child wants to love others as they are loved in this new way."

Dad shook his head. "Holy cow, that explains a lot of why I spent two years in therapy. I didn't really know anything about emotions until I met your mom." Mom joins hands with Dad. "I think the therapist filled the mom and dad receptacle for me, and your mom really helped a lot, too. I didn't realize it, but I hardly ever feel down-deep alone fear, the death type you mentioned."

Sarah goes in for a group hug, tears of joy sparkling on everyone's cheeks, and asks playfully, "Did you guys publish this theory?"

Important Points:

At our core, we all have the same feelings before different thoughts and behavior and feelings occur: Love and Fear along with our five body senses. When this core oneness is made conscious and forged, the potential parent-child bond becomes permanent. Here are the core mechanics.

- Conflict is the welcome bonding home for forging parent/child core feelings.

- "Who I am" is created from deeply rooted shared feelings felt during conflict.

- Fear is deflated and love inflates the "I'm lovable" belief. "I'm unsafe, alone, and wrong" is replaced by "I'm safe, bonded, and OK."

- Bonded children feel basic value and self-confidence, ready to deal with life's differences.

- The bonding "feeling loved" conflict experience is transformed into loving others.

How To:

Here is an inside story from fourteen-year-old Sophia.

I don't know what's wrong with me. When I watch a sad movie, I can't stop crying. Even when there is teasing at school, I feel all tight inside. There's this red-headed girl with freckles that the kids call Carrot Top. There were at least five kids laughing at her, and she just hangs her head. It feels like they are teasing me. I feel so alone and like it's my body that is being made fun of. I know I'm not her, but I can't help it. A lot of times I can't keep my tears back and the other day the teacher asked what was wrong. I told her and she said to try and not let it bother me. I wish it would work.

Then the biggest thing is at home when Dad gets on me about making all A's. I'm in Gifted and Talented classes and really work hard—at least three hours of homework every night. He keeps saying I'm smart enough to get all A's, and on my last report card I did get all A's. I want so badly to please him, and I don't feel I can tell him how worried I am. I can't tell you how scared I get when he asks me, "How's school going?" I'm so afraid that now I'm lying and when I have an overdue paper, before I can stop myself, I say, "It's done." Then I feel so guilty. I don't know why but I'm starting to have stomach aches and some nights I can't go to sleep—I just see Dad's upset face in my mind.

What makes it so hard is that he's always loving to me and calls me his Queen of Queens—it makes me feel so cozy and close to him. Other times we have so much fun. We play father-daughter tennis every week. Yeah, he gets a little picky with me, but we laugh and it's so fun to go out afterwards to have lunch together. But more and more I'm feeling so hopeless, like I'm trapped and there is no way out. Maybe Mom could help. She has answers to everything—well almost.

When I brought it up to Mom she said, "You know all he wants is for you to try your best." I couldn't make myself say what I felt—it would just disappoint Mom. It didn't help a bit what she said. After that I felt even more hopeless, alone and cut off from both Dad and Mom. It's hard to describe but I get a dull ache and a stabbing feeling in my chest. And I can't stop thinking about my Mom's comment and what Dad might say next. Worst of all, every time those thoughts come up, the ache and stabbing in my chest comes back again.

I finally went to my school counselor and told her everything. Wow is she something else. I couldn't believe my ears. She said about twenty percent of people are like me, super sensitive—it's called a Highly Sensitive Person, or an Empath. These people feel everything at a number ten level as if it is happening to them. And usually you can't do anything about it, and you're left feeling it. That's exactly like me. Right away when she explained it, I didn't feel so alone. I didn't feel so different. Yes, twenty percent of people are the same as me. She said she'd call Mom and Dad to recommend counseling. That really worried me, and I told her I was scared Mom and Dad would be mad. I'd rather just leave it alone. I don't want to mess up their lives. Dad's got enough on his plate with possibly losing his job, which worries me a lot. She reassured me they would not be mad and offered to meet with my parents and me to discuss it.

The rest of that day I'm surprised that everyone couldn't see my inside bubbling feeling. Most of me felt so relieved. What if Dad and I could find a way to talk about school without me feeling so scared? The worry would be over. I can't even image that, but the possibility made me smile inside every once in a while.

Fast forward after three LIFT counseling sessions. Here are several highlights.

The biggest thing that happened was that the therapist switched everything around right away. He had me do all the talking and my parents listened. You talk about weird! At first, I kept apologizing every time I said something that I knew would hurt my parents. It took a whole session of practice, but I got to the point that I could talk about it and feel safe. After each point I made, full of feelings, the therapist would say I should have these feelings because they were the deepest part of me, they were not right or wrong. It was hard at first because I could see both Mom and Dad were really bothered by what I was saying, and I just knew I was blowing it.

The therapist asked my parents to share their deep-down feelings and I really got upset. Both my Mom and Dad cried when they told me how upset they were that they missed everything I was feeling. And they eventually said the same thing as the therapist said about my feelings—that I should have been scared and feeling alone and they had no idea. On that last one I immediately felt bad that it was my fault. So, I said it and my Mom and Dad, with the therapist coaching, chimed in that it was their fault for not paying more attention to my feelings.

After the first session, and for sure after the second session, everything changed a lot. To start with, after the first session my dad said he would never again put pressure on me about grades. We agreed that I'd work for at least B's and he asked Mom to monitor him. To tell you the truth, I couldn't imagine this happening. But the little bit of hope gave me that cozy feeling and I felt so close to both Mom and Dad. And after the first session they made a list of everything that was great about me and put in on the refrigerator. Talk about feeling pumped up!

Several other things changed almost right away. Any anger or upset that happened in the future would be handled by them listening carefully to me and agreeing with my feelings and trying to say stuff that proved to me they understood. And the coolest thing—if anyone got too angry, they were supposed to leave and come back when we could talk kindly. Only after that would we find solutions that worked for all of us. Life is so much more fun knowing all this and sharing feelings, and always being accepted by Mom and Dad. I can honestly say, I really like myself and am starting to look forward to improving what needs to be improved, if that makes any sense.

Now it's a month later and I can't believe it—the ache and stabbing in my chest is gone and all my feelings are supported by both my Mom and Dad. And I did get one B+. And my dad hugged me and said, "Ata girl, my Queen of Queens." What's cool is that when one of my parents forgets stuff, the other one will get everything back on track.

The biggest thing is that I feel my Mom and Dad both have my back, no matter what. And what's really cool, I'm getting more confident about myself even when people disagree with me. And my therapist helped me build a plexiglass top for my heart. He had a model of it in his office. I learned that I would always feel what another person felt but two things were important: Stop feeling completely responsible for fixing stuff, and feel alongside other people, not the exact inside feeling of the other person. It's taking a while to get the hang of the last one but when I do it, the relief is great.

Summary:

Parents proving they share the same feelings with their child during differences deflates Fear (feeling abandoned, alone, unsafe, misunderstood) and establishes Love (sameness and oneness) as the endless energy and information source for a full life.

CHAPTER 6

I'm Loveable—Important?

Teach me to be nice to myself when I mess up
so I can be nice to others when there is a problem.

MY TALENTED AND GIFTED (TAG) teacher asked us to write an essay: Is a fifth grader basically bad or good? It sounded impossible but figuring out the answer was a life-changer.

Right away I remembered Nathan, the class bully, teasing a kid with only one arm just before school started today. That's bad. And then I tried to think of someone that was good. There's this fourth grader that invited me to help start a club for collecting canned food for the homeless. It's really been fun to have so many kids bring food in and then go with our parents to the bridge people and hand out the food. Funny—when I thought about both of those kids, I felt tight and stressed about the first one, and so relaxed and like warm water running through me with the other. I'll take the second one any day!

It made me wonder why one person would choose to tease the kid with one arm—so mean—and another think of helping people—so kind? Then I thought about a special series we just finished in our TAG class on emotions. I didn't know it, but what starts when we wake up and ends our day before sleep are four emotions that every human constantly has: fear, anger, sadness, and love. The teacher said love and fear are the main ones. Meanness comes from anger, and kindness from love. Our teacher said *anger is always caused by fear* and we use anger to try to get rid of what's causing the fear. She said it rarely works and almost always ends up with a lot of sadness. Confusing! What would make that bully fearful of the kid with one arm? Who knows? I'll ask the teacher later.

Then I wondered what got that mean kid to be so angry all the time—it's like his full-time job. Also, it seems like more people are mean than loving. Mom probably knows. She's always so loving to me. She's a brain doctor and is also really into religion.

So, I asked her, "Why are so many people mean and so few kind?"

"Do you remember your lessons about the four emotions, especially how fear and love are our two basic emotions? Mean people don't love themselves," she explained. "They think they are bad and have a lot of fear. Kind people really love themselves, feel they are good, and are constantly corralling their fear with love."

"Mom—dumb it down for me. I don't get it."

She pointed to a plaque on the wall above the table—*If you don't have something kind to say, zip it*—and asked me, "What does it take to think kind thoughts and be kind?"

I had forgotten, but now I remembered. The answer comes from a Confucius saying right below the kind plaque: *Never impose on others what you would not choose for yourself.* Duh! Who would choose being mean to themselves?

"You are always helping me to be kind to myself, Mom, especially when I mess up. Now I think I'm getting it. When there's a problem and someone's mad at me, I feel scared. You always say it's natural to be mad or mean to yourself and the other person when you're scared. But as you say, it always makes things worse. I guess that's what makes a person mean to others—being scared. And you've taught me to be kind to myself and not get mad at myself or the other person."

I point to the Confucius saying. "Since I choose to not be mean to myself, I should not impose meanness on others, right? It's hard to always be kind but it really works. Mom, thanks for helping me be kind to myself."

Mom continues, "When that kindness is a habit toward oneself and others, a person knows they are lovable; they like themselves and know they will be loved. It's really possible for everyone, but so few achieve it like you have. So, do you think the bully is kind to himself or angry when he makes a mistake?"

"He's got to be really angry at himself and takes it out on everyone. Is it something like that?"

"You've got it," she confirmed. "Never forget, when you always practice being kind to yourself, in turn you'll be kind to others, and here's the big thing—people will really like you."

I got out of my chair and hugged mom, "Thanks mom, for teaching me to love myself. I'm going to try to be extra kind to the bully." Now I don't dread writing that essay.

That's the remarkable LIFT result with a precious child: "I'm Lovable."

Meanness and kindness: key mechanical points

- *Meanness* results from unattended fear, processed with anger (UMOS, Unattended Mind Operating System), resulting in an attack on self and others. Constant Focus Point splitting.

- The purpose of the meanness is to eliminate conflict-causing feelings of abandonment, aloneness, and splitting from others. But venting anger causes more disconnected feelings.

- *Kindness* is the action of embodied love created by processing fear (COS, Center Operating System) through joining parents.

This creates bonding by forging the Fear Fault Line at the Focus Point.

- Joining normalizes a child's core feelings (body and emotions) during fear-infested conflict. Oneness is the ultimate body and emotion experience.

- The result is the child's feelings of "I'm safe," "I belong," oneness/sameness, "I have value," and eventually "I'm lovable."

- Embodied "I'm lovable" is transformed into selfless love (kindness) for others— "I want others to feel lovable too." Scientific evidence demonstrates kindness is active as early as six months of age. Typically, it is buried before six years of age.

How a child becomes a bully and what can be done about it

Let's first listen in to the feelings and thoughts of Nathan, and then I'll ask his Mom, as well as you readers, to join me in determining how to help him acquire "I'm lovable." Mom will take over in the therapist seat with my coaching. Remember—I promised parents could become their own LIFT therapists.

Just a little heads-up first. Nathan has always been a willful child (personality trait) which means at home he is constantly oppositional and defiant, saying "no" to everything and always arguing a point, even when it does not make sense. It's been that way forever. His parents have all but given up; nothing they do makes any difference. So far, he is not as defiant at school, but he does bully. Now let's listen to his inside thoughts and feelings.

"I get so sick and tired of needing to pick up my room. I can find everything I have by just throwing it in one corner. Mom's always bugging me about picking everything up off the floor. It's a total waste of time. I can sometimes delay by telling her I'll do it tonight. And just now, right before bed I got yelled at for not brushing my teeth and taking a shower. That stuff is just not important. I know she can't make me do it and I'll hold out as long as possible. And since Dad works the night shift, he isn't here to bug me about it.

"What really makes me mad is when Mom reduces my Minecraft time to 45 minutes a night because I don't do my chores and I have so much missing homework. Now that really makes me mad and I don't hesitate to yell and argue with her about it. She says chores are a family responsibility. I really don't care. And taking my dirty clothes downstairs once a week—no way! She's home all day, she can do it. And back to school, I just don't see a purpose in schoolwork, especially history and math. Those subjects have nothing to do with being a fire fighter. That's what I want to do.

"And like things aren't bad enough at home, I get into trouble at school, too, for teasing kids—especially the kid with one arm. They say it's bullying. I know I shouldn't say it and I could never tell anyone else, but it's fun seeing him squirm when I give him a hard time and it makes me mad when everyone pities him so much and are so nice to him. He thinks he has so many friends.

"I don't care about friends anymore. I hate it because I've lost all my friends this year. First, my best friend moved away. And now my parents say I'm not allowed to hang out with another friend who gets in trouble all the time for vaping and stealing and stuff like that. Oh well, who cares? Mom and Dad don't know it, but I like vaping, too, and I might try marijuana. I wonder what's wrong with me that no one likes me? I hate sitting alone in the cafeteria, but I guess I'm getting used to it. The teachers hate me, always getting on me for missing homework. And the principal really hates me. He's always watching me to see if I'm teasing anyone. He loves to lecture me—always the same, blah-blah-blah—then I know I'll hear all about it that night at home. My life sucks!"

That's just a brief snapshot of the typical thoughts running through Nathan's head—Focus Point split, surface (Epicenter) welding never bonds, making everything worse. I don't know about you but my heart aches that an eleven-year-old could be so miserable.

And other than the bullying, his other problem areas are common to lots of kids—no friends, arguing about homework and chores, and feeling misunderstood. So, as my co-therapists, let's dive in and Lift him out of his misery.

First let's answer some important questions about his Center issues and bullying. Don't look at my possible answers at the bottom of the page until you have your answers. Maybe jot down your answers on a piece of paper.

1. What's the condition of his Fear Fault Line and how does it explain his behavior?

2. Fear or Love: What is the percentage of each, inside and outside?

3. Why does he defy and oppose everything?

4. Why does he bully? (Hint: When we feel like we barely exist, it's human instinct to find someone weaker than us and say negative, demeaning things—like making fun of an overweight person.)

Possible answers: (1) The Fear Fault Line is completely split, full of fear and anger at self and others with no chance of recovery. Anger at self and others is instinctual. (2) 100% fear inside and outside; 0% love inside and outside. (3) He is always wrong and never right. To survive inside and hold terrifying fear at bay, he must fight to be right all the time, or take the opposite side from Mom. Every correction from Mom must be met with "she's wrong and I'm right." To agree with her would mean "I don't exist" and would cause more unmanageable fear. (4) At the Focus Point (Fear Fault Line) Nathan experiences himself as a complete failure—totally unlovable, no value, unsafe, and abandoned. His survival instinct is to find someone weaker than him and make that person feel and look as miserable or more miserable than him. Then he feels somewhat superior, or at least less weak, still miserable but alive.

How did you do? I'm sure you got the answers generally within the ballpark. That's all you need to do. Now let's take a quiz on several beginning steps for you to get an idea about what to say to help Nathan begin to feel some value and the beginning of lovability. You'll know the answers immediately and do not need to write them down.

1. Starting point: behavior or feelings (body and emotions)?

2. Engagement process: LOVE (Listen, Observe, Validate, Evoke) or reasoning lectures?

3. Arguing: stay engaged or take a break?

4. Evoking (E letter in LOVE) a mutual solution: chose a 99% successful solution, or "You need to do what a kid your age should be doing"?

Congrats, you graduate with honors! Now we are ready to have Mom dialogue with Nathan, each person feeling they are thoroughly heard (nonexistent with arguing and defiance). LIFT's COS processes ensure what you say or hear is accurately vibrating in your ear drum, and what you mean, or the other person's meaning, is processed at each person's Center. Surface Epicenter exchanges are monologue; usually the ear drums are not activated. Your defense team is busy making battle plans while the other person is talking— that's less than useless Epicenter engagement.

Now I'll coach you on implementing several of the above four points so you can complete your internship. Just a warning with chronic opposition and defiant behavior: the resistance at first is like pounding on steel and the hammer eventually breaking. Do not count on immediate evidence of a breakthrough. But you can count on the COS processes speaking to the core center. You stay focused at the Focal Point Center. The resistance is purely because a lot of cement has been poured over the need to be loved and valued in an effort to cover up the hurt and fear. There is literally no awareness of this basic need. Here's a LIFT guarantee, though: enough focused feelings validation—no mention of behavior—will eventually crack the cement open. "I'm lovable" is down deep waiting to be activated.

Before we get started, review Chapter 2 when Becky's Mom was successful in using LOVE. This exercise will get you started on the right foot and build on this new foundation for further Center dialogue skills. The setting is their kitchen table and Mom is going to engage with Nathan. She will have an earpiece connected to me that Nathan can't see, and I've got a remote pulse monitor to determine when she panics. So, let's do a little prep with some specific guidelines for Mom:

> You know his biggest problem is he feels split from you, alone, abandoned, unloved, and feels misunderstood. So, should we start with a mini lecture or activate the L for the listen part of LOVE? You've got it! You will listen (never interrupt), then do the rest of the LOVE process. Remember, he is only aware of his side of the split Fear Fault Line—it's the starting point. You know all this, but at first it seems unnatural. And here is the biggest problem as he talks: You will want to disagree with him because it is all distorted. But you can't disagree with his feelings—the wielding (forging oneness) at the Focus Point will not bond. You'll need a couple of practice rounds, but here is what you will eventually be able to do.

Enough. Here he comes, frowning.

As he pulls the chair out, Mom says with a smile, "Nathan, I'm always harping on you about everything. That's got to be horrible."

He shakes his head sideways and mutters, "OK mom, what do you want? I need to get back to my game."

"Actually, I'd like for you to tell me how awful your life is around here," Mom says with a smile. Nathan squints just a little bit and mom continues, "I'm just going to listen and try to show you I'm hearing you."

He sighs and tells her, "It's the same old thing. You want me to do stupid chores and I just don't want to, and you can't make me."

Mom asks, "Which is the worst?"

"Well, like my room. I like it the way it is."

Mom responds, "I'd be mad too if I had to do something that was useless."

Nathan slightly tilts his head, squinting his eyes, but rapidly recovers and says, "Yeah, you said it alright—it really ticks me off."

"So, you get mad when I ask you to clean it?" Mom continues.

He answers, "No, duh! Why wouldn't I?"

Mom responds calmly, "Yes, you should be mad." Nathan's surprise is quickly covered up.

Mom says, "I've got an idea for you to think about, if you don't mind not answering now. What if every Saturday I picked up stuff off the floor?" He shakes his head sideways and says, "Whatever."

"And then I thought you should take a break from all chores for two weeks, Nathan."

Now the pause is longer. "That would be the day! That's the way it should be anyway."

She continues, "And for your missing homework, all I'm going to do for the next two weeks is put your missing homework list on your desk on Monday and Wednesday."

He frowns. "You can do what you want but I'm not going to do any of it."

Mom says, "I don't blame you. Tell me some more about how much you hate school."

Nathan opens up just a little. "All my teachers hate me, and math is just too hard." He tells her more than he ever has about his school discouragements, and Mom is continually validating the emotions.

She ends by thanking him for sharing and telling him how she wants to respond with support from now on instead of criticism. And then she says, "We should go to Ben and Jerry's tonight and enjoy some ice cream."

He stares at her for the longest time and then nods his head yes. "If I can get the toppings I want."

That never would have been allowed before, but Mom answered, "You can get any topping you want." Nathan responded by giving her a little half smile.

Good job, Mom! Here are the things you did really well:

- All joining and no splitting through attention to his feelings.
- All listening and validating feelings; no behavior focus.
- No biting at his old bait—negative, angry, rejecting comments.
- All new responses to old surface problems: cease fire on chores, missing homework list only, you pick up the floor.
- Start fun experiences with new twists—ice cream with toppings.

Remember, this is just the start at the Focal Point Split. I can guarantee he is getting the first feelings (body and emotions) that he is valued. As this bond strengthens, you will be able to move into him acquiring more age-appropriate behaviors and respect. This will never happen unless the Center bonding is solid.

Summary point:

Finding and expanding a place for oneness during difficult times guarantees increased Center value experience that will lead to a core belief of "I'm lovable." Kindness to others is always the result.

CHAPTER 7

Better Let Your Teenager Know All About Everyone's CEO "I" and Beliefs "me"

*Listen to and see the deepest part of me
so I can learn to be good.*

GREG'S DAD POINTED TO water coming out of the rocks. We'd been traveling a winding road into the mountains beside the Sacramento River for the last hour. Beautiful!

"That's the headwaters, the first visible beginning point of the Sacramento River. Underground somewhere is the wellspring, the actual source of this water.

"As I was explaining this morning with the PowerPoint slides, each one of us has a headwater called the 'me'—all of a person's beliefs that will determine how we think and act—our special identity. People can see it flowing out of us as we make our way through daily life.

"Each person also has an 'I'—our source or starting point at birth, the unseen wellspring of 'me.' Each 'I' has basic personality traits: quiet/active, positive/negative mood, etc. As life develops, the 'I' does the same thing a CEO does for a company. It oversees and executes everything to make sure the company's beliefs are good and things get done right. The deepest possible 'I' source is the capacity for kindness or love. Science says we are born with it, and its capacity has actually been located in the brain. Six-month-old babies can already start to show love and kindness.

"But there's a problem. On the surface of things, our minds do not automatically attend to unmanaged fear that is always lurking around to get rid of threats. Sadly, for most of us, unmanaged fear buries our 'I.' Our love wellspring is replaced by anger in order to get rid of threat."

He continued, "In this fear situation, 'I' is always in 'fight or flight' mode and uses anger to get the job done. It's miserable and doesn't need to be this way. Most people have an 'I' like this."

Greg's Dad, Howard, sure is smart. He is the CEO of Personal Growth Unlimited. My thoughts were racing, and it was like a light bulb was turning on. Down deep, like in my stomach, I felt more relaxed, maybe in the "Center" part Howard showed us in his PowerPoint. Is it possible my "I" is always fearful, but that's normal? Whew! This warm feeling was the same feeling I get when I go to my grandparents' lake house with them. And come to think about it, there is no fear there. It's all kindness, and so much love.

Let me tell you how this trip with Howard came about. I spend a lot of time at Greg's house. Several weeks ago, I got the courage to ask Greg why he always sees the good in everything, and his parents never—well almost never—get mad at him when there is a problem. Seems like I am always doing the wrong things at home, especially arguing and blowing up, and I can't stop it. I am always thinking, "What's wrong with me?" and recently, "I am bad." I feel scared.

I brought it up to my mom and dad. Dad just laughed and then gave me his stern look. "Yes, you do blow up way too much. You better learn to control it."

Mom was more kind about it. She told me, "Your Dad used to be the same way, but he grew out of it." It's so confusing. I am still scared, and now I feel like I have a bunch of tied up knots pulling tighter and tighter inside of me.

Anyway, getting back to Greg's answer to my questions. He said his Dad taught him about the "I" and "me" inside everyone. It sounded weird to me at first. But now it was really making sense, especially as I was looking at the beautiful headwaters flow. Being together watching this in silence felt so good inside. *Greg and his dad had replaced fear with kindness.* Wow! I really like how that feels.

My thoughts were interrupted by Howard's gentle hand on my shoulder. "Does this make any sense to you?"

Suddenly, tears filled my eyes, and several dripped down my face. I hadn't done that for a long time. Headwaters maybe? "Sorry, I got something in my eye. Yes, it makes sense."

Then all three of us were silent as our attention focused again on the gurgling headwaters making their way to future unknown twists and turns. I felt so relaxed. The beautiful sound made everything so warm, and strangely hopeful. I had a good feeling down deep inside that we all were so together, just like I felt at my grandparents' lake house.

After that life-changing trip, I asked Howard if he could help me and my parents learn about this stuff. He referred us to a therapist that did this new type of therapy: Love Infusing Fear – Therapy (LIFT). We went through the therapy and let me tell you—it changed everything.

"I am lovable" became my "Center" belief. The "me" flowing out of my "I" was so fulfilling.

Key mechanics of "I" and "me"

- "I" is the beginning, center, continuing source of my ever-developing identity— "me."

- I's first experience is body sensations (feelings): unpleasant/pleasant, wet/dry, hungry/fullness, etc.

- I's unpleasant/pleasant feelings are the first "knowing" of fear/safety, a lifelong first "me" sensation/experience—embodied emotion.

- I's feelings are the basis for developing "me," "my" meaning of all life situations.

- "Me" is my identity: all my beliefs, characteristics, and personality traits that show me to myself and others.

- LIFT "me" is marked by humility and joining, grounded in "the sameness in all of us invites kindness," and "I enjoy showing kindness in my own way and respect your way." Safety is guaranteed.

- Fear-based "Me" is marked by separateness. "I am different than you," and "When there is difference, I'll show you I am right." Danger is always lurking around the corner.

Let's see how this plays out in the different stages of a child's life, from a baby's first experiences to a fifteen-year-old boy.

Mia—five days old. Mia is crying because she is wet, and her body is uncomfortable. Mom gently picks her up, holds her within a foot of her own face, and mirrors for several seconds the emotion of unpleasantness. Eyebrows are squinted. Voice tone only slightly tense: "Oh, you are feeling so uncomfortable." Mia is noticing her mouth and eyebrow movements. Mia is physically/experientially taking in mom's reflection of her unpleasantness as "Mom's the same as me." This is the first phase of reduced danger/increased safety and warmth. Immediately after these few seconds, mom starts reflecting safety with eyebrows relaxed, voice tone and mouth soothing while stroking and kissing her check—tight body relaxing. "You're feeling uncomfortable and mommy is changing you right now so you can feel better." Mia physically/experientially digests the reflection and experiences the unpleasantness as something natural that will go away—the final phase of normalizing beginning fear experiences.

This is Mia's first "Love deflating Fear" (body feeling) experience: sameness/oneness/relaxed, mom knows my unpleasantness and it can be fixed.

Summary: All moms have lived this experience. Isn't it one of the most profound life miracles? The developing "I" and eventual "me" starts with embodied first basic fears and unpleasant body/life sensations. They are immediately integrated with oneness, safety, and calm, ensuring minimal Fear and maximum Love sensations, establishing the "I" wellspring.

Caden—two years old. Caden loves his Play-Doh Fun Factory. His temperament tends toward the overt, willful side. Caden always puts up a fight when asked to stop playing. Here is a LIFT Dad handling quite a challenge.

Dad sits on the floor admiring Caden's creation, "Caden, that castle you made is very good. In just a little bit we'll put away..."

"No!" Caden covers the castle with both hands.

Dad points to the highest part of the castle, "Wow, I love how you made those windows."

Caden relaxes, smiles, and points to the horses, "Daddy, look at horses."

They spend several minutes admiring his work and then Dad says, "In just a little bit we need to stop and take a nap." Caden frowns, clenching his fists. Dad continues, "But first let me see you make another horse." Caden smiles, relaxes, and focuses on making another horse during the next several minutes.

"Wow, that's awesome. I really like his ears." Caden smiles and Dad continues, "Now let's go take a nap, I'll put this..."

Caden yells, "No Daddy!"

Dad says, "You should be angry. Play-Doh is so much fun, but now I'll count to three…" Caden yells even more, pounding the floor. Dad says quietly, "I'll need to carry you to your room." He picks him up, still yelling, takes him to his room, and sits in his room while Caden's yelling decreases. He reaches for Caden's favorite Teddy bear, and when the yelling is almost gone, says, "Puggy wants to take a nap with you." Caden frowns, taking several deep breaths, and slowly comes over and relaxes into Dad's lap. Dad carries him to his bed with Puggy while he sings Caden's favorite song—*You Are my Sunshine*. Within several minutes, with Puggy in his arms, he goes to sleep.

Summary: Caden's behavior is normal for an overt, willful temperament. Could you see LIFT being played out? Dad established as much oneness/sameness as possible with a difficult transition. He reflected how awesome his son's creation is and was participating (joining). Fear was normalized—Caden was feeling "I can't ever play with this again." And Dad telling him, "You should be angry." Without anger (that was the hard part) dad brought in the tow truck and delivered Caden to his room without a word. Dad stayed calm, joining with core emotions through and after the anger. Usually parents get angry, lecturing about what's wrong. Caden knows even though "I was angry, and Dad was upset," down deep inside he feels valued and loved (oneness throughout). The developing "me" is feeling safe with fear's anger. He's learning how to acquire regulation—feeling deep inside "I" is normal and OK.

Harper—11 years old. Ever since Harper started sixth grade, she's been crankier and has started to be disrespectful to her Mom. She says things like, "I ought to be able to wear whatever clothes I want," and, "All the other girls get to wear makeup." She's taken a big interest in the latest fads and fashions. She spends a lot of time watching YouTube videos, and has posted some questionable things on Instagram. Harper has become more resistant at any hint of restrictions. When any talk of restrictions comes up, she's angry. "You are way too strict and unfair. You don't let me do anything I want to do." Another thing her Mom has noticed—she's not had near as many sleepover invitations. When asked about it she says, "It's no problem. Who cares?"

Let's listen in to how a LIFT Mom navigates this one.

Mom's new job last year has turned into a sixty-hour work week, and as she reflected on Harper's changes, she realized she had significantly reduced time spent with her. Even when Mom invited her to do something together, there was an increased push back that was never there before. They had always had a lot of fun together. Now, after a few LIFT sessions, Mom knew what to do.

Saturday morning, Mom goes to Harper's room where she is engrossed watching her favorite YouTuber, and says, "Hey Harper, I…"

Harper snarls, waving mom off. "Mom, I'm busy. You always come in at the worse times!"

"You're right, I sure don't pick good times to talk. Can I ask you something before I go?" Head shaking sideways, sighing with a deep breath, she pushes the pause button, "OK, what now Mom?"

"I was thinking it might be fun to eat out at Jose Muldoon's," Mom suggests.

With a contorted face (and thinking *that's my favorite place and we haven't been there for two years*), she stammers, "Uh, yeah, I … guess. Oh, I know, I must be in trouble and you want to break it to me there?"

"No, actually I've been thinking that I haven't been very available to you and I'd just like to have some fun together like we used to." Harper jerks her head sideways and squints unbelievably at her Mom. "How about tomorrow around two?"

Harper stops to think. *That's Sunday. We've never done anything like this on a Sunday. This is weird.* She responds, "OK Mom, I'll take you up on it. Can we stop at Sonic afterwards for a malt, like we used to?"

Mom gives a thumbs up. "You're on."

Fast forward to Sunday at the restaurant. "Harper, I can't tell you how cute that blouse and dress look on you. And where did you get the idea to curl your bangs like that?"

"I saw it on YouTube—Ella Victoria. I watch her every day and …." Harper stops and looks deep into Mom's eyes. "Are you going to put me down if I tell you about it?"

Mom reaches out to cover her hand, which Harper still accepts, and says, "From now on, I'm going to do a lot of listening and hardly any talking. I really can't wait to hear more. And when we get home, maybe you could show me one of her videos."

Harper can't hold back her smile and shifts in her chair, bending forward, "Mom are you kidding? What's happened to you? You have barely talked to me since you started that dumb job last year."

Mom tears up and reaches for a napkin. "You are right, the job has put blinders on me. I've not only been disagreeing with you on almost everything, but I've really been frustrated a lot and always trying to correct you."

Harper's eyes well up. She fights back the tears and cannot talk, her body feeling warmth like she's in a hot tub.

Mom continues. "From now on, every time we disagree, I'm going to listen to you so you feel understood. If you are up to it, can we start to go out to lunch once a week?"

Harper looks confused, but manages to get out, "O…K."

The rest of that afternoon they talked about fun memories, specifically their last Christmas at Grandma's house, and how she had hired a cowboy duet to perform just for their family. And how Grandma took her on a shopping spree like no other. They giggled together about a lot of things. And afterward, the malts from Sonic tasted great.

During the next week, Mom made a point of watching Harper's favorite YouTube videos. Harper then opened up about some stuff she had felt Mom didn't have time for. The group of girls that were her friends are now getting into sex and vaping and she had to choose for now to have no friends. Once Harper shared all of this, she could hardly stop crying and it didn't take Mom long to join her tears. Together they decided she could join the local tennis club where there was a great program that included monthly parties. Harper loves tennis and got very excited about getting involved and meeting some new friends.

Summary: The "me" was dominated by fear, distancing her from her wellspring "I." Mom's LOVE oneness did the trick. The "I" was reconnected and once again became her source for the healthy evolving "me."

James—Fifteen-year-old freshman. By the second quarter of his freshman year, his parents noticed James was changing. He was complaining about not being able to get to sleep until two in the morning. Even melatonin didn't work as it had in the past. He seemed to get frustrated easier, and when asked about it he said he didn't know why, but "there's nothing wrong."

He started worrying about things more, too. Even though he wanted to take the AP chemistry class, he was now worried because his grade was a B. He usually got straight A's. He also had started dating and some bullies at school had put false information about him on Instagram about sexual stuff. His parents knew this had to be painful because James was such a sensitive boy. When his parents tried to show their support, he said, "It's no big deal. I can handle it myself." His parents stopped asking, thinking he needed his independence. On top of that, during the past year Dad had lost his job and there was a lot of money tension and talk about needing to possibly move.

Here is how James' parents connected after only two LIFT parenting sessions.

Sitting around the table one evening eating mom's cherry pie with ice cream, James's favorite-of-favorites, Dad said, "James, Mom and I are feeling sad about how you are doing. We..."

"Dad, there is nothing wrong. No reason to feel sad. Is this going to take very long? I have stuff to do." His eyes welled up as he shifted around in his chair and took an extra-large bite of pie.

Mom told him, "Dad and I have been talking and we realize Dad's job thing has got to be really difficult for you. And I know this Instagram stuff has got to be..."

The tears now drip off his cheeks as he pushes away the Kleenex Mom tries to hand him. "I've just got something in my eye."

Dad continues, "The other thing Mom and I realized is that..." James pushes his chair back and runs down the hall to his room.

Mom and Dad wait and then go to his room, finding him sobbing on his bed. They haven't seen James like this since his dog had to be put to sleep two years ago. They sit down, and mom says ever-so-gently, "I'm so relieved you are letting your pain out." Before LIFT training, she would have said, "We're going to get through this," or, "Dad will get a job soon—you let us worry about that."

James sobs even more. Dad lets the silence be comforting and then gently says, "I am so sad..." His voice trails off. James takes a quick glance, sees his dad wipe tears away from his eyes and thinks *I've never seen him cry except for a minute at his mom's funeral four years ago.* His body feels like ice water, thinking: *Now I've really ruined everything. Could something awful happen to him right now?*

Dad reaches out to pat James on the shoulder. James feels a bit uncomfortable because Dad has never done this before, but a certain warmth starts to flow through his body. He allows the touch as his Dad haltingly tells him, "I love you so much. I can't remember when I've told you that." James glances at Mom, who's also crying. And suddenly both parents lean over to him and hug him. He sits up on his bed and they all hug each other, patting each other on the back.

Now James says, in between sobs, everything that has been bothering him: AP class, social media bullying, and how he feels almost constantly afraid that he can't handle all the stuff going on. And reading between the lines was, "I felt you guys were so busy that I didn't want to bother you with my stuff and make everything worse."

Before LIFT, Mom and Dad would have interrupted, out of love, and given him reassurance that "Things will get better—we'll get you a tutor." Now they were addressing his deep-down Fear with comments like, "That's so sad," or "Is this what you are saying?" And then making validating comments. "We've not spent near enough time with you, which will change today," and, "It's OK—you should be feeling all these things."

At one point toward the end of their conversation, Dad pulls out his phone and starts typing in a scheduling entry. "Let's do a weekly tour of all the best hamburger places in town." James is a hamburger junkie.

James chuckles, "Dad you're kidding—really? Aren't you too busy and wouldn't it cost too much?" Dad smiles like James has not seen for a long time. "No son, from now on I'm putting my time and money on you. Everything else comes second."

James hugs Dad again, "Dad, I love you." He didn't even know where that came from except it felt like that gusher at Yellowstone that they had visited—it just gushed out and was it ever warm and powerful.

Summary: By now you can recognize all the LIFT parts and the sheer joy and contentment of what it delivers. Do you hear James's "I" shattering the "me" that got so disconnected from his Center?

On a personal note, it's only in the past several years of my practice that I've put LIFT through its paces. I've been privileged to witness the breakthrough of tears and hugs in my office as families have courageously allowed Fear to deflate and allowed native Love to flow. There is never a session when this happens that I do not tear up myself. What an inspiration those families are to me as I witness how the Center "I" of a child is always eagerly waiting to be awakened.

CHAPTER 8

I'm So Grateful for LIFT Parents: A Millennial's True Confessions

LIFT Love Live: Becoming me is so exciting

JUST LIKE YOU, I'VE read all the chapters in this book. I could identify with every one of the stories because I'm a LIFT-raised kid. Now I have my first job—yes, you guessed it—I'm interning as a professional counselor. I'm also navigating out of a two-year relationship that didn't work out and trying a couple of the online dating sites. That's the ultimate LIFT test. Later, I'll tell you more.

I'd like to share some highlights of my life. "The proof is in the pudding," as my beloved Grams used to say. I'm here to tell you I've not only tasted the LIFT pudding from the get-go, but it is my diet for life. I'm hoping you can get a feel for it by the time I'm done telling you my story.

So here it is in one sentence. (Steve Jobs, are you proud of me?)

Complete awareness and acceptance of *inside* fear and love *feelings* increases the highs and makes the lows great opportunities to know me better.

Did you see Super Bowl LIV and that twenty-four-year-old hero's performance? Patrick Mahomes's two interceptions were transformed into back-to-back touchdowns including a perfect 49-yard pass in only eight minutes. What's his secret? "I just try to be the best I can be."

Wow, what an inspiration! Here's my LIFT interpretation of Mahomes:

**I really have good value ("I'm lovable" or "my best") and
I turn up its flow (infusing fear) when I'm scared.**

That was exciting for me to hear because that's the sentence that started coming out of me about halfway through my 6th grade year.

Here's my story. During my senior year, I was in Advanced Placement (AP) Math and English and usually got A's, or an occasional B+. But over a one-month period, these classes became really hard for me and I got several C+ grades on my assignments. I was really scared. When my mom and dad got wind of it, they both did what they always did, mostly my mom. I could tell my home-builder dad had to sometimes work at it. But since I was Daddy's girl—no problem.

"What are you feeling?" I was used to all the feelings talk from Mom and it always had been comforting in the past. But for some weird reason, this time I couldn't get the word "scared" out, when before it was always easy to admit to her.

"I'm OK Mom, don't worry." I can remember I felt tense getting the words out.

Mom gave me her gentle titling-head look and, touching my shoulder, softly said, "Sometimes we have difficult experiences and our mind says, 'something's really messed up about me.' That's just natural fear telling you something isn't going right. The 'something not right' is the situation—not you." That was mom doing the cool LIFT —validation. It made sense but I couldn't shake the fear. It didn't feel like the fear was going away.

Then I heard her say, "Maybe we could get a tutor..."

"No, I know I can do it." I turned and went to my room to watch some YouTube.

Anyway, fast forward one month: I just couldn't get on top of the classes, or feeling like something was wrong with me, and I landed in our family therapist's office. Our whole family has had an annual checkup with him for as long as I can remember. Here's what I found out.

Up until this school problem, I enjoyed life and really liked me. As long as I can remember, my parents made fear as common as fast breathing, always validated by mom and dad as normal. I can vaguely remember having a lot of temper tantrums when I was a little kid. Dad would say calmly, "I know you're afraid you'll never get to finish your Lego creation and you're angry and yelling." Building Legos was such a fun thing to do with my dad. "Let's go play in your room so the anger can calm down." It took a lot of time—probably a year—doing this, but it eventually worked where I learned to use emotion words instead of yelling. I know it sounds unbelievable, but eventually I would just go to my room myself.

Anyway, back to what the therapist helped me see and feel. My Center likable self was slammed with the C's. I was truly scared there was something wrong with me. I was feeling so hopeless about life and like such a failure. I had even been thinking about vaping and maybe hanging with the kids in my class who were dabbling with drugs. Would that make me feel better? Within several therapy sessions I could see clearly what was happening. No, something wasn't wrong about my Center—fear had just taken over. Knowing this opened my "likeable me" door and it began lighting up everything again.

Here's the upshot of that experience. I accepted, along with mom and dad, that "doing my best" probably meant shooting for C's in those AP classes. It didn't matter what everyone else did. I knew what my best was and now I knew what to try for. I was back to living from my long-time established "lovable Center" which had always been my parents' focus for me.

I never really understood completely what had happened until I wrote about it in my graduate school autobiography. The science part is interesting. I hope you think so too.

Fear's constant nanosecond readiness requires constant outside and inside Pure Love action: validation/normalization of feelings, both physical and emotional, as well as noticing any images that come along with it. There are two triggered stages when threat happens. *Inside Stage 1* is the inside meaning a person attributes to the threat. Without healthy outside validation, the meaning is typically "I'm wrong, I'm bad and unsafe." This meaning is placed into our databank for future reference. Anger is triggered either toward one's self or toward others as a way to defend through Fight or Flight response. Then there's the *Outside Parenting Stage 2*—the outside meaning designed to deal with the faulty Stage 1 meaning.

There are two Stage 2 options:

1. Parents focusing only on outside behavior which always results in the child's feeling "I'm wrong, I'm bad."

2. LIFT's Pure Love focus on validation of fear, resulting in a healthy fear meaning: "It's normal, I feel safe, and I'm OK." Healthy solutions always occur.

When LIFT parenting Stage 2, option 2 happens regularly, "I have good value" is eventually established in the child's databank. It morphs into an intended core human belief of "I'm lovable." As a LIFT child gets older, often by six years of age, the outside Stage 2 parental validation becomes integrated into a child's initial Stage 1 way of dealing with a threat. When a threat happens you have natural fear, but then you quickly validate the emotion the way your parents have done. You sidestep the awful "I'm bad" and instead feel "I'm OK."

Here are the inside mechanics. After you've integrated your parents' fear validation, the instinctive nanosecond Stage 1 "I'm unsafe" threat is transformed by Stage 2 integrated Pure Love "I'm lovable" thoughts. Raw fear will always be our first instinctive first Stage 1 responder. But then Stage 2 takes over without needing parental involvement: "The fear I feel is normal. I'm safe and I know I can find a way to handle this. Most of the time I don't feel alone. Mommy and Daddy feel the same way and always help me solve stuff. Even when I'm at school and something happens, I can feel Mom's touch, her smiling face and kind voice. And Dad is smiling, nodding his head in agreement." Bottom line: Your body is calm, emotions are positive, and images are soothing.

One critical developmental "wiring" fact in closing: A child becomes what they hear, see, and feel from parents. I want to say "thank you" to my Mom and Dad for the "I'm lovable" mirror they always put in front of me!

It helped me to learn that by about age five the body sends chemical signals: cortisol's cold stress, and the opposite warm contentment from the attachment chemicals—oxytocin, endorphins, dopamine, and serotonin. It was at one of our first family annual therapy checkups that we learned about this in more detail with special breathing exercises to turn off stress and turn on the warm chemicals. Our whole family practiced this special breathing often, even during good times. I'd say all of us did it at least several times a week. I can still remember Dad doing several deep breaths when I argued with him.

So, you're probably thinking this sounds too good to be true. You're not alone. Out of my grad school class of 25 students, I'm the only one who had parents like mine. I was grounded in "I have good value," no matter what. And if you're feeling uncomfortable because you don't do all these things—don't. You've already qualified as a loving parent or you would not be reading this. LIFT therapy works remarkedly well no matter when you start. Remember, deflating fear releases Love' abundance.

It's one of those situations where "too good" was actually a regular occurrence. And it's not me. It was my parents fully implementing the 21 LIFT Pure Love Habits which we will get to right now. (See list in Appendix I)

Unproductive Fear can't exist with Pure Love's continual validation practice.

Isn't it interesting how all major religions and spiritual traditions say, in one way or another, this same thing? I can't figure out yet why mainstream psychology hasn't jumped on this Fear/Love concept as central to everything. You'd think professionals would take a hard look at the "psych" part of their "psychology" profession and take seriously its root meaning—soul or spirit, which LIFT labels "Center." Most scientists acknowledge our unseen, unconscious part—the 95 percent that runs everything—is still quite a mystery. But I think LIFT points us in the right direction.

Just one more fascinating thing that happens with LIFT that is hard to explain but always happens: **A parent's selfless validating becomes a part of the receiver, who eventually wants to be selfless toward others.**

Here are the 13 basic Pure Love Habits:

1. Humility

2. Feeling validation

3. Giving loving kindness

4. Gratitude

5. What's right—not what's wrong

6. Emotional literacy and fluency

7. Vulnerability comfortableness

8. Inside to outside transparency

9. Mindfulness breathing

10. Owning my part of a problem first

11. Forgiveness

12. Listening first

13. Reconciliation (discussion procedure)

Unproductive fear doesn't have a chance in a LIFT family. Hallelujah!

As I have said, my parents practiced Pure Love Habits in our home as I was growing up. The thing I remember most is the big four-by-six-foot whiteboard with all our names listed at the top. Each name had a heart drawn around it, and the title written on the board was "We value others and ourselves equally." Each month one of us could draw our customized emoji next to the title. Mason, my older brother was always finding new ones that were so fun.

Underneath each name was a special trait noticed by family members. When I was four, my trait read "enthusiastic" and my brother's trait was "creative." Traits were added as family members saw them emerge. It's funny how just writing "enthusiastic" still fills me with excitement and warmth. I just have to say it—Love is so cool! I didn't know it then, but the hallmark LIFT habit of validation was doing its "I'm loveable" work. You'll sense this habit working underneath almost all of the other habits.

One of the most fun things I can remember is the last Friday of every month we had an ice cream party to talk about each one of these traits. We also shared the biggest success we each achieved during the month and it was written on the board underneath the trait. Add ice cream to attachment chemicals—now that's a party!

Half-way down the left side of the board was a heading "Gratitude," and several spaces down "Giving," personal (weekly) and family (once every two months). Every Friday we had a special meal at which time we each shared what we were grateful for. I can remember being so surprised about what Dad or Mom would say. One I can remember so vividly from Dad: "My mom and Dad putting up with my constant hyperactive stuff." And Mom saying one time: "My Dad having monthly dinners out with me when we got all dressed up." I didn't know it then but remembering this is such a good feeling.

Each week at our Sunday family meal we had to tell one family member what we would give them, or how we would do something nice during the next week. You can imagine this took some training from Mom and Dad, but you'd be surprised at how easy it soon became. I'll never forget when I was in the first grade and I couldn't think of anything. Mom suggested thanking a family member at least one time during the week.

The family giving to others once every two months included things like taking a meal to an older house-bound person or maybe shoveling snow off someone's sidewalk as a surprise. I can remember at first it was boring, but then I started looking forward to it. Now I know why—I had such a secure feeling doing something together as a family. And I also got to enjoy a lot of warm responses we got from people.

Writing things on the whiteboard was fun. I found out in my neurology class that writing things down and drawing visuals make things stick in our minds better. I can still visualize the board and in my mind see and hear those meal discussions on giving and gratitude.

On the bottom right side of the board we could put up our favorite photos—two from each of us. It was especially fun when we put family vacation photos up there. I can remember often standing there enjoying the pictures. We were able to take one vacation a year. Sometimes it was close by for several nights at a hotel with a swimming pool. And then every few years we got to go somewhere out of state. We'd decide where we were going on our trip months ahead and put pictures of the place in that section of the whiteboard.

If you haven't gotten the drift yet about my personality, remember that tantrum story. Well, to put it mildly, it took a lot of practicing to change my willful personality. Mom and Dad really worked hard with me to establish "using words" for my feelings. I can remember as early as four years of age being able to say regularly, "I'm angry," or "I love you." And then maybe by five or six, staying calm enough to work out alternatives to yelling. That's the emotional literacy and fluency skill working which automatically gets you into the transparency habit—showing what's inside calmly so people see most every part of you.

As a side note, most self-help books and workshops address how vulnerability is a given and needs to be pushed through. With LIFT, the vulnerability comfortableness habit is a given because there's barely anything to hide due to emotion transparency. LIFT continually sooths fear—vulnerability's biggest scare. With little to no fear, vulnerability goes out the window, but never too far away.

Back to how Dad and Mom helped me with my willfulness. They always listened first, repeated what I said, and asked if they heard it right. Then they always agreed with something I said—the "what's right" habit. After that I can remember the solution usually included my point. You guessed it—that's the "reconciliation" habit. I really got good at this by the time I was in middle school.

After solutions were in place, I'd be encouraged to practice the "owning my part" habit. Often, I'd argue about cleaning up my room. They really got good early on at stopping the arguing and asking me what my part was—after I calmed down. Here's where I was encouraged to practice the mindfulness breathing. Eventually I got the point. By about the fourth grade I got the blaming habit down: stop blaming others and see my part when a problem came up anywhere. The rule in our family was when there's a problem, start with your part first. Now I'm amazed at how rare that habit is in peoples' lives. When you look at your part of a problem first, there's very little left about what's wrong in the other person.

One other thing related to the reconciliation habit: Mom and Dad always demonstrated the forgiveness habit. Maybe they had yelled too much or dropped into picking on my behavior instead of looking at feelings first parenting. They always told us they were sorry. Hearing them say that regularly eventually rubbed off on us and soon it became a habit for both my brother and me. Of course, it took some practice.

I remember wondering why my family was always making such a big deal about feelings and I recall an event when it really started making sense. It was a bright Saturday morning, and Dad was taking me with him to visit one of his construction sites. It was just after my first week in fifth grade and it was so cool to be able to go with him. We were walking down into the freshly dug foundation of a new house he was building. The earth smell is still with me matching tingling warmth. I'm still amazed at how the memory works, with both body senses and images.

I don't know why but I remember something just popped out. "Why do we do all the feelings stuff? I don't know any other kids that have a big whiteboard like us."

He pointed at the foundation trench: "The ground is like us at birth, all ready to build ourselves into adults. The earth must be dug up just right so when the cement is poured everything is level and a good solid home can be built. It takes about nine months."

"Same with babies. They get built into adults. The beginning earth trenches and cement are like our Love and Fear emotions, our ground and foundation that's there from the beginning. Getting the mix of Love with Fear just right from birth on builds the best adult possible." He tilted his head, blue eyes shining while ruffling my hair, "And from the looks of things the mix has been perfect." I couldn't help it—I jumped into his waiting arms.

"You know how I was looking at those big sheets of paper, the plans for this house in my pickup? Well, that's what our whiteboard is. It's the building plan for our family we follow every day. The Love and Fear emotions 'cement mixer truck' is happening every minute of every day and needs careful attention."

It was like a light bulb turned on. But the best part was our trip home and stopping for several pieces of turtle chocolates.

During my college years I reflected a lot about our family dynamics, and it started making a lot of sense. I was feeling valued through validation. Just recounting it makes me feel warm and happy. Now I know that's Pure Love flowing inside me.

You notice I haven't mentioned humility, the first habit in the list. To me, it's the natural result of the other 12 habits being practiced consistently. Now I can see it is humility that's behind the title on our whiteboard: "We value others and ourselves equally." For me, the top six humility habits are feeling validation, own my part of the problem, giving, gratitude, reconciliation, and forgiveness. Of course, none of these would be effective without emotional literacy and fluency.

So, in closing I want to share how all of this works with the dating situation I mentioned in the first paragraph of this chapter. My two-year relationship ended like this. He said to me, "You always asking how I feel just doesn't work for me, especially when you want to know right away. You've really tried to stop but it's still too much." There were other things, but this was the big one.

At first when I heard it, inside me felt like a 7.9 earthquake with a −30° wind chill. Inside Stage 1 thoughts were racing out of control like the Indy 500: "It's bad that I'm so feelings-oriented. This is all my fault. I'll be all alone now." —on and on. Then halfway around the track the cautionary yellow flag came out and inside Pure Love Stage 2 started with purposeful breathing and getting paper and pencil out to journal. My energy and information sources were switching from fear to "I'm lovable." Journaling gives you a chance to see your inside often hidden feelings on the outside by writing them down. Scientists say it's almost as good as counseling. The coldness inside started subsiding as "I'm lovable" began to cautiously peak around the corner. Here's the gist of what I wrote on and off during that first day, mostly Pure Love Stage 2 thoughts.

I should have been scared and sad. Then I addressed being alone. Yes, that's scary because we are meant to be in relationships. But being alone will help me know a little more about my good stuff and improvements I can make—this ain't my first rodeo. [My grandpa used to take my brother and I to rodeos and it was a lot of fun.] One spiritual guru said half of who we are is unknown and when we are alone, we get a chance to know more of ourselves. Count on it being scary at first. The next day I talked to my mom and she reminded me that relationships are about goodness of fit, and my boyfriend's puzzle piece didn't fit in a feelings-focused relationship like I want. Even though I had heard this before, this comment started to dim fear as I realized "it takes two to tango."

Of course, there were ups and downs after that and I decided to deal fully with the grief of loss with several sessions with our therapist.

One last point: LIFT pulls off experiencing oneness, especially when there is a problem. I found out in my studies this basic point—everyone yearns for oneness, that "you are the same as me" feeling, especially when there's upset. Dousing sustained Fight or Flight and maintaining minimal cortisol is definitely the way to go.

And then there are the experiences with dating sites. I'll leave that for another time, but it is definitely serious fear fault line territory.

So, what's the takeaway from my LIFT experience?

Soothing my felt fear first ensures life's intended meaning.
I love treating others the way I treat myself.

21 Pure Love Habits

Inside Pure Love good habits

1. Humility: equal concern for others and me

2. Feeling validation

3. Vulnerability comfortableness: gateway to oneness, humility transparency practice

4. Transparency, Center emotions open to others, flows through humility

5. Emotional literacy and fluency

6. Truthfulness

7. Listening first

8. Reconciliation (empathic listening to opposing points leading to mutually agreed upon solutions)

9. Owning "my part of a problem" first

10. Forgiveness

11. Mindfulness purposeful breathing and "now" focus

Outside Pure Love good habits

12. Giving lovingkindness

13. Gratitude

14. Knowing and practicing "my purpose"

15. Independence

16. One-on-one parent time

17. More free play time than screen

18. Noticing what is right more than what is wrong

19. Opportunities for improvement replace mistakes

20. Regular nature exposure

21. Exercising

<u>New Courses Now Available!</u>

Gary Unruh, MSW brings over 50 years of counseling using the LIFT method that has transformed thousands of lives.

Gary now offers step-by-step courses on applying the LIFT method to improve your personal and family relationships. Take you and/or your child's personal development to the next level.

Send all inquiries to this email address:
garyunruh@gunruh.com

Made in the USA
Coppell, TX
23 February 2021